a passion for
poetry

practical approaches
to using poetry
in the classroom

by Mandy Tunica

PRIMARY ENGLISH TEACHING ASSOCIATION

The views expressed in this book are those of the authors and do not
in any way reflect the opinions of the Primary English Teaching Association,
its Board or its staff.

First published September 2005
by the Primary English Teaching Association
Laura Street, Newtown NSW 2042, Australia
Tel 61-2-9565 1277
Fax 61-2-9565 1070
Email info@peta.edu.au
www.peta.edu.au

Copyright © Primary English Teaching Association 2005

Tunica, Mandy
A passion for poetry : practical approaches to using poetry
in the classroom.

Bibliography

ISBN 1 875622 61 6.

1. Poetry – Study and teaching (Primary). 2. Poetry and children.
I. Primary English Teaching Association (Australia). II. Title.

372.64

Illustrations by Terry Denton
Cover and internal design by Jane Cameron, Fisheye Design
Edited by Kathy Prokhovnik
Printed by Ligare Book Printer, Riverwood

Contents

Foreword

When in 1954 I arrived in London for the very first time, I had one thought in mind. I asked the taxi driver to take me to the College via Westminster Bridge and to stop there awhile. On a clear morning I got out, walked onto the bridge and spoke aloud: 'Earth has not anything to show more fair ...'. As I came to the final lines of Wordsworth's sonnet I silently uttered a prayer of thanks for Miss Fox. I could – and can – still hear the timbre of the voice of that remarkable teacher from 20 years before. In the discussion that followed I became aware for the first time of imagery, of personification. Now, another 50 years on, I frequently take an early morning walk across the Tarban Creek Bridge. I stop, gaze across at the city skyline, and again quote Wordsworth; and bless Miss Fox. Such is the sustaining power of poetry; and such is the inestimable influence of a wise and committed teacher like Miss Fox, and like Mandy Tunica.

My first introduction to poetry was in the cot as my mother shared nursery rhymes with me. Then in the Infants' Grades we were blessed with the Green and Brown Readers with poems like Christina Rossetti's 'The wind has such a rainy sound,/Moaning through the town'; William Blake's 'The Piper and the Child' that dances in the mind, leaving an indelible trace-mark. And on Wattle Day, I still sing words from the Brown Reader, 'The bush was grey'. I give thanks regularly, too, for Mr Roland, the teacher who had Year 3 kids learn and recite M Forrest's 'Boy Dreams' and Henry Kendall's 'September in Australia' – which I recite every spring. How pallid and depleted my life would have been without such a legacy left by wonderful teachers! A week before my father died in his late eighties he was still reciting poetry.

Little wonder, then, that I tried as a young teacher and later as a college and university lecturer to model myself on teachers such as Mr Roland and Miss Fox. But it took other enthusiasts such as Mandy Tunica years along the track to alert me to the joys of verse writing in the classroom; or to the expressive value of choral (or verse) speaking: Lydia Pender's dramatic 'There are bunnies about' or Dorothy Simmons's 'Puppies for sale! Puppies for sale!'

I am grateful to Mandy, too, not only for her teaching strategies but for her recognition of the place for, at times, the deep study of a poem. The love and the joy of poetry is enhanced as children – and adults – come to appreciate the form and structure of a poem, the poet's artistic expression of experience, use of imagery, and of rhythm and rhyme – or the flow of free verse. So much depends on the teacher and Mandy Tunica has so much to offer us all. Back in 1996 she inscribed my copy of *For the Love of Poetry* and I still value and refer to that inspiring work that was born of her enthusiasm for and dedication to the unique place that poetry can play in enriching the lives of the children for whom 'only the best is good enough'.

Then, after all that has been said about the 'teaching' of poetry I am mindful of Eve Merriam's injunction in her 'How to Eat a Poem': 'Don't be polite/Bite in/Pick it up with your fingers and lick the juice that may run down your chin/It is ready and ripe now, whenever you are'.

So eat up: sometimes slowly and reflectively; sometimes just gobble.

Maurice Saxby

In Praise of Mandy
(with apologies to Henry)

Our Mandy's gone to battle now
Along the Queensland border
She's toiling hard for every bard
And so we must applaud her.

At Byron Bay amid the spray
Or up at Noosa Head
We hope she's well; there's much to tell
To keep us poets fed.

Our Mandy's gone a-roving now
From Nhill to Narromine;
From Young to Bourke, she's hard at work
Across the land of Strine.

By riverboat where Lawson wrote
And Murray cod dive deep,
By billabong of that old song
Where waltzing swagmen sleep...

Our Mandy's gone a-roving now
And if you chance to meet her
She'll say it's time to quote a rhyme
So hail the power of PETA.

With spark and speed she takes her creed
And roams around the nation.
Her words will reach the brave who teach
The younger generation.

Where poets reel and lack appeal
With not a contract handy,
From Hume to Hay, it's time to pray
That heaven sends us Mandy.

Max Fatchen, November 1996

Preface

My love affair with poetry began when, at a very young age, my somewhat eccentric mother read me *Hamlet* (the entire play in instalments) passages from *King Lear* (especially those relating to ungrateful daughters!) and a few Shakespearian sonnets. Oh, how I yearned to hear an Enid Blyton story! My early love of words and their sounds was developed by a primary school principal who passionately recited 'I think that I shall never see/ A poem lovely as a tree' and 'I must go down to the sea again, to the lonely sea and the sky/ And all I ask is a tall ship and a star to steer her by'. Although I was never asked to memorise any of the poetry of Shakespeare, Kilmer or Masefield, I am still able to recite lines from them all. Sadly, I cannot remember one poem nor one English teacher from high school — although I dimly recall paraphrasing Shakespeare. Fortunately, my love of poetry was rekindled at university where I couldn't get enough of Auden, Yeats, T.S. Eliot and Judith Wright. However, it was only when I began teaching and began searching for poems to use with my junior classes that I began to appreciate the richness and variety of this precious lode of literature.

This book could not have been written without the support and encouragement of many people. I wish to thank those members of the PETA Board who believed in the need to publish a book on poetry 'teaching' and who invited me to write it! Thanks also must go to Anita Ray for all her early efforts, David Smith for his constructive advice and Kathy Prokhovnik for coming to the rescue when I was 'drowning'! Once again I am indebted to the Australian 'teachers', Vivienne Nicoll-Hatton, Moira Robinson and Sean Monahan, Rory Harris and Peter McFarlane, whose ideas and approaches have had a significant influence on my thinking, and their English counterparts, Michael Rosen, Charles Causley, Aidan Chambers, James Britton and Andrew Stibbs. I also wish to thank my long-suffering family who have had to drop everything and listen to yet another 'old favourite' or a newly discovered poem being read aloud. The book is enhanced by Terry Denton's whimsical illustrations. Finally, may I thank all the superb poets (dead and alive) whose words inspire me and live on in the corners of my mind, and all the wonderful school students whose enthusiasm for reading and writing poetry continues to delight me. Special thanks to the students and teachers of Collarenebri Central School, Annandale North Public School, Warrimoo Public School, Blue Mountains Grammar School and St Paul's Primary School Moss Vale.

Although I grow old (I have not yet worn my trousers rolled!) I have lost neither my passion for poetry nor my deep faith in teachers to teach poetry in such a way that their students will voluntarily read poetry for the rest of their lives.

Mandy Tunica

Introduction

This book is written for teachers to assist them revive the flagging fortunes of poetry in schools. By focusing on enjoyment and by promoting a love of words and sounds it is hoped that they will develop students' life-long interest in this literary genre.

The ideas and opinions expressed in this book are based on my observations as a teacher and school inspector, and my more recent experiences conducting poetry workshops in schools across NSW. Some of the stimulating ideas are borrowed from other teachers, poets and writers both in Australia and overseas.

The various chapters address different ways of using poetry to promote reading and responding, speaking and listening. In order to redress the current imbalance in school writing programs where transactional writing seems to be the norm and poetic writing the exception, I have included two chapters on poetry writing. Teachers can just 'lift' some of these units and put them in their programs. While some of the teaching approaches and resources may be more suitable for younger students and some more appropriate for older students, almost all of them can be adapted to meet the needs of age groups from five to fifteen years. After all, poetry is not age-specific.

Since poetry, like all the arts, is a very personal matter, my selection of poems reflects my own taste. Although I have included some 'wacky' poems which appeal to children, other poems are included purely because they are my favourites or because they wear well. The bias towards Australian poems can be justified on the basis that they are as good (or better) than those from other countries and often provide a unique insight into our history and culture. Also, by wide reading of poems written by Australians (be they white, Anglo-Celtic, Aboriginal or relatively new arrivals) we can hopefully earn them all a few dollars! The poems written by students are liberally scattered throughout the text to demonstrate just how powerful their voices can be.

It is worth noting that this book reflects my own personal philosophy about teaching and learning. I am well aware that some of my opinions and approaches will not find favour in some quarters – especially as, although I can mix it with the best of them, I have deliberately abstained from using current educational jargon and vogue words. I make no apologies! If classroom teachers use just some of the ideas and poems to gain a few converts to poetry, I will be happy.

1

The Place of Poetry in Schools

The poet's eye, in a fine frenzy rolling,
Doth glance from heaven to earth, from
*   earth to heaven;*
And as imagination bodies forth
The forms of things unknown, the poet's
*   pen*
Turns them into shapes, and gives to airy
*   Nothing*
A local habitation and a name.

A Midsummer Night's Dream Act V, Scene 1

William Shakespeare

Poetry has extraordinary power. As a kind of word magic it can, in the hands of a skilful poet, affect the reader/listener both intellectually and emotionally. Not only can it reveal profound truths, 'probe your soul', delight and enchant but it also has the capacity to surprise, provoke, astonish, disturb and even enrage us. Its "spontaneous overflow of powerful feelings" (Wordsworth) can also produce physiological reactions such as laughter and tears: a chill down our spine, a catch in our throat and even a pain in our stomachs! Perhaps Emily Dickinson best described the unique power of poetry when she said:

> If I read a book and it makes my body go so cold no fire can ever warm me, I know that is poetry. If I feel physically as if the top of my head were taken off, I know that is poetry.[1]

Art and music can evoke similar emotional responses but they do not, like poetry, use language, which is after all the normal currency of exchange in the classroom.

Poetry and Prose

Although English curriculum documents mandate the teaching of various literary genres, most teachers (K-10) tend to focus more on prose texts (picture books, short stories and novels) than on poetry. While prose writing may at times be 'poetic' it is important to ensure that you provide a balance of literary forms in your teaching program. You should consider the following differences between prose and poetry.

- The distinguishing quality of poetry is that its highly compressed nature makes words work harder. Whereas readers of prose may have to read numerous sentences, paragraphs and pages to experience a certain feeling, a poem which "sits distilled to spareness"[2] can provide a more personal, more immediate response. Arguably, one good line of poetry can offer more insights than a whole page of prose.

- The original and often unexpected combination of words in poetry demands a special kind of attention and provides a different sort of pleasure. As Coleridge once said: "prose = words in their best order; poetry = the best words in their best order".

- Unlike prose, poetry often breaks the conventional rules of writing. When they abandon the established conventions of punctuation, spelling, sentence structure and capitalisation poets entice the reader to play a very different game with words.

- Poetry at its best picks up nuances and thoughts in a way that prose can never quite match.

- Poetry often relies on a higher level of suggestibility than prose. What is left unsaid is often as important as what is said. As the poet Eleanor Farjeon says:

Not the fly, but the gleam of the fly;
Not the sea, but the sound of the sea;
Not myself, but what makes me
See, hear, and feel something that prose
Cannot: and what it is, who knows?[3]

The Value of Poetry

The richness and variety of poetry ensures that it has something to satisfy every reader. In just one general anthology you are likely to find poetry of all kinds from all periods – short, humorous poems, long narratives, gentle lyrics, superb nonsense verse, nursery rhymes, limericks, haiku, riddles, parodies and epitaphs. And the poetry you find may well be, like all human nature, "profound and shallow, sophisticated and naïve, dull and witty, bawdy and chaste in turn".[4]

Poetry has so much to offer students of all ages, abilities and learning styles that we cannot afford to deny children ready access to it. It can and does:

- Stimulate and strengthen the imagination by constantly providing novel ways of articulating experience. Poetry lets the reader's imagination fly free and children are so ready to use this faculty. It is not, as Shakespeare suggests, the exclusive preserve of lunatics, lovers and poets!

- Force the reader to think differently and flexibly or as Aidan Chambers says "subvert the narrow conditioning that asks us to think in a routine fashion".[5]

- Foster skills of speculation and problem-solving often through what the poet leaves unsaid.

- Lead students to appreciate beauty (aesthetic value) by 'communicating the wonder that underlies the familiar and the beauty in the commonplace'.

- Make a vital contribution to language learning. Through reading poetry students learn to appreciate the imaginative force of words as well as their infinite possibilities. Apart from enriching and extending their language, poetry may help them to use language that is more precise, appropriate and deliberated. This understanding can influence the poems they write themselves, and spill over to prose compositions, essays and reports.

- Develop and improve reading and vocabulary skills of students whose first language is not English. While they may not have the skills to tackle long and more complicated pieces of prose they can read and enjoy a short, simple poem.

- Provide success for readers with learning difficulties. They can read and perform several short poems whereas they may find longer prose works to be daunting in that they require a longer attention span.

- Allows students to explore feelings about themselves and link their experiences to their inner selves.

- Satisfy a need to come to terms with the realities of our experiences. Poetry does not ignore the grimmer aspects of our existence and the many modern poems that deal with subjects such as family conflict, separation, death of loved ones, bullying and anorexia can help students cope with disturbing events in their lives and make them feel less alone.

- Lead to a life-long feeling for music particularly when students experience the words and sounds of poetry being read aloud or when they 'perform' poetry themselves.

While it is true that picture books and novels share some of these aspects, poetry is able to visit a wide variety of worlds in a comparatively brief reading time. The impact of poetry is immediate.

Why is poetry so often neglected in schools?

It seems rather ironic that, at a time when poetry is enjoying great success in pubs, poetry clubs, festivals, writers' centres and on the internet, it is being increasingly ignored in schools or as Max Fatchen suggests "is being paddled into some kind of literary backwater".[6]

Of course there are many enthusiastic, talented teachers who love poetry and teach it extremely well. Sadly, however, evidence collected in reports and surveys conducted in the UK in the 70s and 80s[7] which found that poetry was in a general state of decline in schools is as applicable today as it was thirty years ago. My own informal surveys have revealed that many teachers just do not like poetry or are in some way 'afraid' of it. Unfortunately, George Orwell's observation that the mention of poetry is more likely to disperse a crowd than a whiff of grapeshot would probably still ring true in many school staffrooms.

That poetry is being 'overlooked' in schools is also reflected in the current lack of demand for anthologies of poetry for children. Australian publishers seem reluctant to print or reprint such anthologies. This disturbing fact is evident in the lack of general poetry collections entered for consideration by The Children's Book Council of Australia's annual awards. Although the verse novels of Steven Herrick are thriving there is still a disappointing dearth of general (particularly Australian) anthologies. Even when such anthologies are published booksellers seem loath to stock them. Next time you visit a bookshop check out how much shelf space is allocated to children's poetry.

There are also very few serious reviews of children's poetry. Compare the column space devoted to reviewing the ubiquitous *Harry Potter* with new releases by Australian poets such as *Spiky, Spunky, My Pet Monkey* by Doug MacLeod.[8] Refer to any book containing critical essays on children's literature and you will be fortunate to find even one chapter that deals with poetry. Australian writers, such as Moira Robinson and Sean Monahan, have published superb books full of imaginative ideas on teaching poetry, but their titles soon go out of print.

Some years ago I organised a Poetry Festival and invited a whole host of Australian poets to attend. On a glorious summer's weekend in Sydney, Max Fatchen, Bill Scott, Elizabeth Honey, Steven Herrick, Michael Dugan, Anne Bell, Di Bates, Bill Condon and Celeste Walters read poetry and inspired small groups of children to write their own. Whatever the reason – the venue, the timing, the cost or a complete lack of interest – teachers stayed away in droves!

In some ways it is easy to understand why teachers remain unconvinced about the importance of poetry in the school curriculum. Faced with continuous changes to an already overcrowded curriculum, changing methodologies and technologies and constant political debates about 'standards,' 'testing' and 'literacy' they have become seriously stressed. Their morale has also been adversely affected by the poor press they so often receive and the way in which 'the community' expects them to 'solve' all the ills of a modern society.

There are, however, other reasons for the neglect of poetry.

- Teachers' own negative experiences of poetry in school (with its over-emphasis on analysis and interpretation) have 'turned them off'.
- A widely-held view that "poetry is a closed language accessible only to the initiated".[9]
- A perception that poetry is in some way socially irrelevant. This is interesting when one considers how quickly people turn to poetry for special occasions such as weddings and funerals.
- A belief that poetry has little utilitarian value. As John Keating told his students in *Dead Poets Society*[10] ... it won't help you get a job. However, it could be that one of its greatest values lies precisely in its lack of utilitarian value!
- Syllabuses which focus on functional models of language and factual text types and pay scant attention to poetry. It appears that facts and objectivity are valued more highly today than imagination and emotion. Judith Wright, for one, argued that poetry is being crushed by the material demands of society and a too practical approach to education.[11]
- Words like 'joy' 'delight' and 'pleasure' as well as concepts such as 'creative imagination' (all fundamental to poetry) are rarely mentioned in English curriculum documents – presumably because they are too difficult to assess. Maybe it is time to move poetry out of the subject English and into the Creative Arts where it probably more rightfully belongs! Or make it an elective like Art and Music in the senior years of schooling.
- Poetry requires contemplation, plenty of time to muse, puzzle and reflect, and our education systems currently do little to encourage this – "too often stillness is equated with indolence, quietude with laziness".[12] It is indeed a pity that, in today's schools, our students are not provided with more time to just "stand and stare".[13]

Surely, it is time to reflect on where we are and where we should be heading. Have we become too obsessed with assessable outcomes? Have we become blinded by the so-called 'advantages' of functional models of language and formulaic text types? Have we let a certain rigidity creep into our teaching practices and, in the process, lost sight of the individual and his or her emotional needs? Perhaps it's time for all teachers to read Bruce Dawe and heed his message.

teaching the syllabus

Teaching lions to leap through flaming hoops
  Teaching baby elephants to waltz
Teaching dogs on bikes to loop-the-loop
  Teaching chimps to undo nuts and bolts

Teaching doves to pick out painted numbers
  Teaching hawks to sing
Teaching bears the latest Latin rhumbas
  Seals the Highland fling

Teaching those with wings to walk up mountains
  Teaching those with feet of lead to fly
Tossing coins into intermittent fountains
  Calling in the plumber when they're dry

And lastly – when it seems that each performer
  Has learnt the lot – to teach them one thing more,
The thing that in the process they've forgotten:
  Dogs, to bark again: lions, to roar … '

Bruce Dawe[14]

Poetry in Schools

Regrettably, because of the way it is taught in schools, poetry makes very few converts – that is, students who read poetry after school. Rather than encouraging students' open and honest responses to poems teachers are routinely expecting them to complete worksheets, answer comprehension questions (often in "concentrated assaults upon single poems on single occasions"[15]), engage in colouring-in activities or use poems for handwriting practice. There is no doubt that such teaching practices deaden rather than enliven students and do little to generate interest, pleasure or understanding.

Senior secondary students are frequently 'loaded up' with biographical and historical information as well as critics' (aptly described by Coleridge as failed poets!) opinions to supposedly assist them understand a particular poem. Personally, I have yet to be convinced that knowing that a poet loves soccer, food or opium, eventually found God or used a particular rhyming scheme ever added anything to my appreciation of the beauty of the words and sounds.

Although primary school teachers are more likely to read poems to their classes, there is still considerable cause for concern at this level. Reports on primary education in England found that poetry was only irregularly heard by students and that the majority of primary school students did not voluntarily read poetry in school, or out of it.[16] When it was used in class it was generally introduced only as a stimulus for language work. Although poems have occasionally appeared in Basic Skills Tests, probably with the very best of intentions, I fear that young students might forever associate poems with 'tests'.

Probably the most vocal critic of the way poetry is taught in Australian schools was Judith Wright. She was so alarmed by all the letters she received from students (and teachers!) seeking explanations of the meanings of her poems that, at one time, she went as far as to ban her anthologies from the prescribed reading lists. She cited 'Bullocky' and 'Legend' as examples of the way her poetry has been over-interpreted or misrepresented. "I wrote 'Bullocky'," she said "because of a nice old man I knew who I wanted to perpetuate but I now find that it is being blown up into a kind of justification of the whole invasion of Australia".[17] In 1966 she wrote, "'Legend' is a simple poem built on more or less classical fairy-story lines but students obviously believe that it is *too* simple: a trap is suspected!".[18] No doubt Judith Wright would agree heartily with Jean Cocteau's sentiment that "the worst tragedy for the poet is to be admired through being misunderstood".[19]

Another Australian poet, Bill Scott, agrees with Judith Wright. He believes that all children "should be encouraged to read; to hear, enjoy and share poetry" but because of the way it is 'studied' in schools it would be better, he argues, if it were not 'taught' at all.[20] Others, such as the playwright Peter Kenna, have expressed no objections to their works being studied in schools because as he said "We get all that money!".[21] Nor does Bruce Dawe mind his poems being included in prescribed reading lists, although he does admit that "sometimes I've been credited with greater profundity than I really have".[22]

There is no doubt that the final secondary school examination has an insidious grip on the teaching of poetry in the senior years. Well-intentioned teachers prepare their students by having them answer 'trial' questions. To illustrate how obtuse such questions can be one has only to hear how John Misto was baffled by such a question on his play *The Shoe-Horn Sonata*. He recently described how he gave a talk on his play to 200 final year students who asked him to answer their trial examination question. He said "When they read it out, I didn't have a clue!".[23]

As a school inspector, I was fortunate enough to observe a range of superb teachers in action in classrooms. I was, however, greatly disturbed by some of the comprehension questions which were set on various poems. The following examples are included to remind teachers of what **not** to do!

On Bruce Dawe's 'heat-wave':

- How does Davey Boyd die? ('smashed up in a car' was not an acceptable answer!)
- How would you describe the weather on the day he died?
- How was he kept alive for three days?
- How did the author hear about his death?

On Oodgeroo of the tribe Noonuccal's 'Then and Now':
- To which race of people does the poet belong?
- What are lubras? Why did they dig yams?
- List the major changes which have taken place in the area.

On Ted Hughes's 'Thought-Fox':
- Pick out the half rhymes.
- Comment on the different rhythm of each quatrain, the use of sentence and punctuation.
- Why is the use of the hyphen significant in the title?

Also, I well remember an incident described to me by one high school teacher. While 'studying' T.S. Eliot's 'The Love Song of J. Alfred Prufrock' her students asked her who the 'you' was in 'Let us go then you and I'. Her response, 'probably the reader', was immediately written by the students on to the poem. Some weeks later her class attended a study day at a local university where an academic said that the 'you' was Prufrock's *alter ego*. The students were devastated – betrayed by their own teacher!

The last word on how a poem can be mistreated in schools rightfully belongs, I think, to the poet.

The Maelstrom

The waters of indifference,
contempt and derision
swirl and surge on our feeble
poetry lessons.
The poem, a delicate coracle
is battered, bruised and abused.
The tell-tale sneers from peer to peer
force us into the maw
Of turbulent failure.
Around
    and around
        and around we swirl,
frantically struggling to keep
our coracle afloat;
its delicate sound and rhythms
pummelled to oblivion.
Their waves quash the coracle's sides;
and scorned violently
    from the centre
the flotsam eddies near the classroom window.
The lesson
   is
     over.

Kevin O'Connor[24]

The Role of the Teacher

There is no doubt that the teacher and the importance of his or her personality is the vital catalyst in all learning but, in the words of one enlightened educational authority (albeit in 1955!): "perhaps the importance of the teacher is nowhere as great as in the teaching of poetry".[25]

As a teacher of poetry, you should:

- Be a reader of poetry. Buy or borrow an anthology, place it beside your bed and vow to read a poem a night. If you are not already an addict, you should soon 'get the habit'!

- Practise reading aloud. Read regularly to your partner, your children or a friend and share your responses.

- Learn at least one (preferably Australian) poem off by heart so that you can 'perform' it for your class.

- Communicate a simple, personal enthusiasm for poetry to your students. If, after reading and sharing lots of poetry, you still lack any genuine enthusiasm for the genre, have another teacher who is a poetry lover take your class for some of the lesson each week. The English poet Charles Causley believes that if you don't have any feeling for poetry "it's a terribly dangerous thing to try and teach children".[26]

- Be seen to value poetry as highly as spelling and mathematics.

- Create a positive, 'poetic' learning environment to promote enjoyment.

- Encourage the reading of poetry by being seen to read it yourself, talking about poetry by talking about it yourself and writing poetry by writing it yourself. Unless you do this you will run the risk of being seen as "a tailor's dummy in a nudist colony – very bad manners".[27]

- Involve parents and carers in your poetry adventures. Rather than send home a prose 'reader' send home poems to be read and shared. Invite family members to read their favourite poem to your class.

- Try to rid yourself of 'teacher guilt' or what Moira Robinson refers to as the Puritan Work Ethic "which has always been very keen on *usefulness*, on *worthiness* and *work*".[28] Expose your students to a wide variety of poetry, provide ample time for thinking, contemplating and reflecting and numerous opportunities for reading, speaking and writing poetry – no tests, no comprehension exercises, no homework!

Finally, remember that if we continue to ignore, mistreat or misrepresent poetry "humanity will be diminished and the barbarians will have won yet another, perhaps final, victory".[29]

References

1   Cited in *Metaphor* (1999) ETA (NSW) p13.

2   Hay, A (2000) *The Secret*. Duffy & Snellgrove p112.

3   Farjeon, E *Blackbird has Spoken*. MacMillan. Reprinted courtesy David Higham Associates, London.

4   Auden, WH and Garrett, J (1935) *The Poet's Tongue: An Anthology chosen by WH Auden and John Garrett*. G Bell and Sons.

5   Chambers, A (1985) 'Inside Poetry: A shared adventure' in McVitty, W (ed.) *Word Magic: Poetry as a shared adventure*. PETA p26.

6   Children's Book Council of Australia (SA Branch) Inc (1997) *Newsletter*; May:58 p1.

7   The Bullock Report, *A Language for Life* (1975) and the NCTE Report (1988)

8   (2004) Puffin.

9   Britton, J (1983) 'Reading and writing poetry' in Arnold, R (ed.) *Timely Voices: English Teaching in the Eighties*. Oxford University Press, Melbourne.

10   Peter Weir (1989)

11   Wright, J (1966) 'The Role of Poetry in Education'. *English in Australia*; June:2 p97.

12   Allen, J & Angelotti, M (1982) 'Responding to Poetry'. *New Essays in the Teaching of Literature. Proceedings of the Literature Commission Third Internationl Conference on the Teaching of English, Sydney Australia 1980*. Australian Association of Teaching English p167.

13   Davies, WH (1871-1940) 'Leisure'

14   Dawe, B (1997) *Sometimes Gladness. Collected Poems 1954-1997*, 5th Edition. Pearson Education Australia. Reprinted courtesy Pearson Education Australia.

15   Stibbs, A (1981) 'Poetry in the classroom', *Children's Literature in Education*:40.

16   *Primary Education in England, A Survey by HM Inspectors of Schools*. (1978) DES.

17   Interview with Marian Theobald *Sydney Morning Herald* 28/10/83 p4.

18   Wright, J *op.cit.* p98.

19   *Le Rappel a L'Ordre* (1926)

20   Wright, J *op.cit.* p105.

21   Marian Theobald *op.cit.*

22   *ibid.*

23   *Sydney Morning Herald* 28/5/2005 p11.

24   *Spring Poetry Festival* (1983) SAETA p5.

25   Victorian Education Department

26   Merrick, B (1995) 'With a straight eye: an interview with Charles Causley', in Fox, G (ed.) *Celebrating 'Children's Literature in Education'*. Hodder & Stoughton Educational, London (originally published in no. 70, 1988) p88.

27   Stibbs, A *op.cit.* p49.

28   Robinson, M (1985) 'How not to "Teach" Poetry' in McVitty, W (ed.) *Word Magic: Poetry as a shared adventure*. PETA p43.

29   Scannell, V (1995) 'Poetry for children', in Fox, G (ed.) *Celebrating 'Children's Literature in Education'*. Hodder & Stoughton Educational, London (originally published in no. 67, 1988) p97.

2

Reading and Responding to Poetry

The long-term goal of poetry 'teaching' is not to have students just recite a few poems at school assemblies nor to analyse a particular poet's techniques but, rather, to develop a life-long love affair with poetry. To do this, we need to expose our students to a wide range of poetry, focusing on the pleasures of the words and their sounds and, through the processes of reading and responding, developing a 'poetic consciousness'.

Starting Out

Before beginning any poetry-related reading, listening, talking or writing 'activities', try using some (or all) of the following teaching strategies.

- Find a 'work bag' and carry it into the classroom. Tell the students that you are a plumber who has come to fix the broken toilet and ask them what 'tools' you have in your bag and what special skills you possess. You may wish to repeat the performance several times impersonating a variety of tradespeople such as carpenters, electricians or mechanics before you introduce an artist who has come to paint your portrait. Finally, the poet enters and the same questions are posed.

I have found that young students begin by suggesting very basic tools such as paper and pencils before realising (with some prompting!) that the poet's tools are words and his/her special skill lies in his/her ability to use the words in an unusual way. Fortunately, there is always one student who mentions 'imagination' as a poet's skill and so we conclude that poetry is about words and imagination.

- Ask your students the question 'What is poetry?'. Since they are all familiar with picture books, simple chapter books or novels, and since they agree that authors also use words and imagination, I ask them what makes poetry different and then write **all** their answers on the blackboard. You will probably get answers such as 'it rhymes', 'it has short lines', 'it is serious' and 'it's boring!'. Write these responses up on butcher's paper and display them on the classroom wall. As the students are introduced to lots of poems, ask them to remove, amend or add to their original opinions.

- As a fun activity, ask them how they would identify a poet in a crowd. They usually tell me that he (rarely is 'she' suggested) would be wearing 'daggy' type clothes, would have a beard and would be poor! Many think he would not be in a crowd since he would be dead! Show them photographs of some living poets to dispel their misconceptions.

- Ask your students what they think poets write about. You may find that some typical responses include 'love' 'animals' 'countryside' 'daffodils' and 'the seasons'. At this point I read a few poems about death, war, school, bullying, walls and noses. Usually, at least one student will proclaim that 'poetry can be about anything at all'.

- Conduct a quick survey, either orally or as a written questionnaire, of the students' experience of poetry. Questions you could ask include 'can you remember a poem that you have enjoyed?', 'what made it memorable?', 'how were you introduced to this poem?'.

Selecting poems to read with your class

Although the concept of 'immersion' has fallen into educational disrepute in recent years, most writers on children's literature still insist that 'drenching' or 'saturating' students in poetry is the only way to foster enjoyment and appreciation of this literary genre. It is important to remember that poetry is not age-specific. As the poet W.H. Auden said:

> It must never be forgotten that while there are some good poems which are only for adults, because they presuppose adult experience in their readers, there are no good poems which are only for children.[1]

His sentiments have been echoed by many modern poets such as Adrian Mitchell, who points out that "the same poem may mean one thing when you're nine, another thing when you're nineteen and yet another when you're ninety nine".[2] With these comments in mind, we should be wary of underestimating the capabilities of young children, who "need just as much 'grist and gristle' to sustain and purify their imaginative diet as any adult".[3] We should avoid patronising students by selecting poems that we consider to be appropriate to their age level. Remember that children, as E.B. White noted, "love words that give them a hard time providing they are in a context that absorbs their attention".[4]

Although you might start with poems that are short, simple and humorous and that relate directly to the experiences of your students, you should widen their imaginative diet by reading poems that tax their intellect as well as their emotions. 'Poems' that rely on hackneyed lines, absurd rhythms and cheap rhymes may interest and amuse students but they do little to develop a student's appreciation of genuine poetic works. This is not to say that what teachers deem to be 'rubbish' should be banned. Peter Dickinson believes that every diet needs a certain amount of roughage and it is often in the process of reading such 'poor' verse that students will (through comparisons with 'quality' poetry) learn to critique.[5]

Starting where students are at

In choosing poetry, it is essential to acknowledge the wide range of ethnic, religious and cultural backgrounds of our students and recognise the realities (eg. single parent families, death of family members etc) of their experiences. So, it is important to select poems that:

- arouse curiosity;
- speak to students' experiences, addressing food, families, school, friendship and bullying (see Chapter 6);
- demonstrate the strong similarity of poetic thought across cultures on themes such as families, school and animals (see Morag Styles, *I Like that Stuff* and *You'll Love this Stuff*);
- provide an Aboriginal perspective, for example in Rebecca Edwards and Janelle Evans *Crow Feathers: An Indigenous Collection of Poems and Images*;
- have been written by children, for example in the *Special Forever* anthologies published by the Primary English Teaching Association, The Taronga Foundation Prize *Poems by Young Australians* and those published in this book;
- provide different perceptions of the same topic, such as Judith Wright's 'Magpies'[6] and Colin Thiele's 'The Magpie'[7];
- are lyrics of popular songs with meaningful words, such as Bob Dylan's 'Who Killed Davey Moore?', John Lennon's 'Imagine' and Pete Seeger's 'What Did

You Learn in School Today?'. The lyrics to these and other songs can be found in some general anthologies of poetry, including *The Kingfisher Book of Children's Poetry*;

- relate to various curriculum areas, such as Ian Serraillier 'The Will' and Michael Rosen 'Boyfriends' for Mathematics, Steven Herrick 'Science', David Campbell 'Windy Gap' for Geography, or poems from Allan Wolf and Greg Clarke *The Blood-Hungry Spleen and Other Poems about Our Parts* for Physical Education and Health;
- relate to things they will see on an excursion, such as 'animal' poems before going to the zoo, epitaphs before visiting a cemetery as part of a local history unit, war poems before visiting the Australian War Memorial and Aboriginal poems before a visit to an Aboriginal resource centre or Aboriginal site;
- have been chosen by poets. *101 Favourite Poems: Poets Pick Their Favourite Poems* is a useful resource as the poets have selected their own favourite poems and also explained why they like them;
- illustrate the universal appeal of poetry. Read a poem chosen by a prominent Australian − for instance, a scientist, politician or doctor (some are collected in *A Return to Poetry 2000: Ten Australians Choose Ten of Their Favourite Poems*).

Building Personal and Library Poetry Resources

Every teacher needs to have a personal poetry library and the following titles are suggestions for starting your collection. Although some of these books are relatively costly they are all well worth the financial investment! There are some inexpensive ways of building up your collection − add some titles to your Christmas or birthday list, or haunt second-hand bookshops and garage sales. You can also find bargains in new and second-hand books on the internet.

Build up the school library's poetry collection. Ask your school librarian to allocate funds specifically for purchasing poetry books for the school library.

Full references for the following books can be found in the Bibliography.

- A 'good' treasury, such as *The Hutchinson Treasury of Children's Poetry*, *The Walker Book of Poetry for Children* or *Collins Treasury of Poetry*. Treasuries contain hundreds of contemporary and traditional poems of different forms and styles from a wide variety of poets. Also, because they are usually arranged in themes or in general age groups they provide an invaluable resource for locating and reading poems for all occasions. My only reservation is that, although a few Australian poets such as Max Fatchen sneak in, these treasuries are disappointingly 'light on' in the area of good Australian poetry.

- *100 Australian Poems for Children* is an excellent collection and redresses this imbalance in treasuries.
- *Beetle Soup: Australian Stories and Poems for Children* skilfully blends stories and poems and contains some of my very favourite Australian poems. It is now available in paperback!
- Since the preceding two 'texts' focus on contemporary Australian poets, it is essential that you purchase an anthology that includes traditional Australian poetry and particularly bush poetry, such as *Waltzing Matilda meets Lazy Jack*.
- Sharon Creech's *Love That Dog* is an invaluable resource. Not only does the writer provide a variety of poems to be read aloud but she also illustrates ways to promote student response and student writing.
- *Kick in the Head: An Everyday Guide to Poetic Forms* is one of the most beautiful books I have read and, apart from providing teachers with unobtrusive definitions of poetic forms, it includes unusual and interesting poems from a wide variety of poets as examples of each form. The colourful illustrations in watercolour, ink and torn paper virtually leap out at the reader. Although the book is compiled and published in the United States, our own Steven Herrick gets a mention!
- *From Mouth to Mouth: Oral Poems from Around the World* is a wonderful collection of oral poetry from different cultures.
- *The Kingfisher Book of Children's Poetry* has over 250 contemporary and traditional poems from a wide range of poets, representing almost all poetic forms and styles.
- *The Puffin Book of Utterly Brilliant Poetry* focuses on the poems of ten popular, modern English poets. What makes it such a useful resource is the 'interview with the poet section' which precedes the poems of each writer. Students will enjoy the insights that these provide into the poet's attitudes to everyday life and to their art.

Building Poetry Resources for your Class

It is important to provide numerous opportunities for students to independently select and read poems and to browse through a range of poetry books. To do this, you will need to provide some resources.

- Build up a class collection of poetry books so that each student has at least two or three books from which to choose. Rather than spending a lot of money, bring in your poetry books, ask other teachers to lend you theirs, invite students to bring their own and arrange a bulk loan from the school library. Once students have compiled their own anthologies, they can use these as a class resource. A class 'poetry file' can also be developed.

- Apart from general anthologies, it is important to include single author titles by poets such as Steven Herrick, Max Fatchen, Colin Thiele and Michael Rosen.
- Obtain a copy of Gary Crew *Troy Thompson's Excellent Peotry Book*.
- Ensure there are copies of books with bright, colourful covers and intriguing titles, such as Benjamin Zephaniah *Talking Turkeys*, Michael Dugan and Doug MacLeod *Out to Lunch* (also has a tape), Jack Prelutsky and Peter Sis (magnificent illustrations) *The Dragons Are Singing Tonight* and *Monday's Troll*, and Colin McNaughton *There's an Awful Lot of Weirdos in Our Neighbourhood*.
- Keep several copies of Roald Dahl *Revolting Rhymes*, C.J. Dennis *Hist*, Alfred Noyes 'The Highwayman', A.B. (Banjo) Paterson 'Man from Snowy River' and 'Clancy of the Overflow', Gillian Rubinstein *Sharon, Keep Your Hair On*, John Foster (ed.) *Word Whirls and Other Shape Poems* and Doug MacLeod *Spiky, Spunky, My Pet Monkey*.
- Thematic poetry books are useful, such as Grace Nichols *The Poet Cat*, Adrian Henri *Spooky Poems*, Doug MacLeod *Sister Madge's Book of Nuns* and the updated version of Jez Alborough *Guess What Happened at School Today*.
- Keep a class set of at least one verse novel, such as Steven Herrick *Jim Jones Saves the World*.

Although I love Charles Keeping's haunting, evocative drawings for 'The Lady of Shalott' and 'The Highwayman', Brian Wildsmith's bright, beautiful illustrations in *Mother Goose: A Collection of Nursery Rhymes* and Chris Raschka's bold, striking illustrations in *A Kick in the Head*, I personally find most illustrations distract the reader from the poem and interfere with imagination. Some are unnecessary, inappropriate and tend to trivialise the poems.

Selecting Poems from Various Poetic Forms and Styles

As well as poetry such as nursery rhymes, parodies, limericks and riddles, a poetry reading program must include poems from the three great styles of poetry – the dramatic, the narrative and the lyric. Although, for convenience, I have generally listed poems according to a poetic form, it must be remembered that there is considerable overlap between the styles. Also, while it is important that students experience traditional forms and styles, it is a good idea to share poems that do not follow traditional patterns.

The Bibliography provides a comprehensive list of useful anthologies and books by individual poets.

Nursery rhymes

There is no better place to start young students on their exploration of poetry than nursery rhymes, especially as many of them may not have experienced them at home. Nursery rhymes with their phonological patterns of alliteration and rhyme play a crucial role in children's early reading success, and their relatively complex grammatical structure, compression and paradox contribute to their general linguistic development. However, they do so much more than this. In Maurice Sendak's words, "their elusive, mythic and mysterious elements"[8] transcend the nonsense and provide the reader with an emotional as well as an aesthetic experience. Since their themes are so diverse they not only teach children some very basic facts of life but also satisfy their curiosity about the essentials of human experience.

Consider the themes that the following nursery rhymes touch on:

- 'Where are you going to, my pretty maid?' (courtship)
- 'Cock Robin and Jenny Wren' (marriage)
- 'There was an old woman who lived in a shoe' (poverty)
- 'Solomon Grundy' and 'Who Killed Cock Robin' (death)
- 'One I love, two I love' (courtship)
- 'Three blind mice' and 'Ding, dong, bell, pussy's in the well' (oblique aggression and cruelty)
- 'One, two, buckle my shoe' and 'One, two, three, four five, once I caught a fish alive' (counting)
- 'Thirty days hath September' (days in the months)
- 'Monday's child is fair of face' (days of the week)
- 'Hey diddle diddle' (distinguishing between sense and nonsense)
- 'If all the world were paper/And all the sea were ink' (speculation).

You can use collections of nursery rhymes, such as:

- Benjamin, F. (ed.) (1995) *Skip across the Ocean: Nursery Rhymes from around the World*
- Faustin, C. (ed) and Toft, L. (ill.) (1994) *The Kiskadee Queen: A Collection of Black Nursery Verse*
- Opie, I. (ed.) and Wells, R. (ill.) (1996) *My Very First Mother Goose*
- Torres, P. (1987) *Jalygurr: Aussie Animal Rhymes*
- Wildsmith, B. (1987) *Mother Goose: A Collection of Nursery Rhymes*.

Parodies of nursery rhymes

Having read the original nursery rhyme to your class, you should read some parodies. After all, what better way is there to get into the original form? Children love the humour (often bawdy) and the unpredictability of the parodies, which so often reflect the inventive word play, bizarre violence and bawdiness of their playground poetry.

Little Miss Muffet
Remains on her tuffet
And hasn't been frightened away.
The spider, down-hearted
And dizzy, departed
Repelled by her pressurised spray.

Max Fatchen[9]

Pussycat, pussycat where have you been,
Licking your lips with your whiskers so clean?
Pussycat, pussycat, purring and pudgy,
Pussycat, pussycat, WHERE IS OUR BUDGIE?

Max Fatchen[10]

Mary had a little lamb
A little pork, a little ham,
An ice-cream then some soda fizz,
And boy – how sick our Mary is!

Anon

Humpty Dumpty sat on a wall
Humpty Dumpty had a great fall.
All the king's horses and all the king's men
Had scrambled eggs for breakfast again.

Anon

Incy Wincy spider
climbed up the waterspout.
Down came the rain
and washed poor Incy out.
Out came the sun
and dried up all the rain,
so Incy Wincy spider
climbed up the spout again.
Remember this poem
any time you might
be tempted to think
that spiders are bright.

Michael Dugan[11]

Monday's child is red and spotty,
Tuesday's child won't use the potty
Wednesday's child won't go to bed,
Thursday's child will not be fed.
Friday's child breaks all his toys,
Saturday's child makes an awful noise.
And the child that's born on the seventh day
Is a pain in the neck like the rest, OK?

Colin McNaughton[12]

A useful resource for parodies of rhymes is *Mixy's Mixed-up Rhymes* by *Mixy* (with help from Richard Tulloch).[13]

Parodies of poems

Parodies of well known poems are also popular. *Mad* magazine often parodies poems (along with everything else!): this one is from the 1970s.

Kubla Khan

In Xanadu did Kubla Khan
A stately pleasure-dome decree
With marble bathtubs in each john
And evr'y room a great salon
To please his family.[14]

Other parodies include:

- Bernard Stone, 'The Charge of the Mouse Brigade'[15]
- Michaela Morgan, 'Blake's Tyger – revisited'[16]
- W.C. Sellar and R.J. Yeatman, 'How I Brought The Good News From Aix To Ghent Or Vice Versa'.[17]

Parodies of songs, carols and hymns

Advance Australia Fair

Australians all eat ostriches
For we are young at three.
With Go Dance Oil
And Well Foot oil
Our home is dirt by sea.

Our lamb abounds
On nature strips.
Our beauty rich and Andrea.
In joyful trains then lettuce sing,
Advance Australia Fair.

Elizabeth Honey[18]

The following parody of the well-known Christmas carol 'When shepherds watched their flock at night' was written by a group of young children.

While shepherds washed their socks by night
All seated round the tub
A bar of Sunlight soap came down
And they began to scrub.[19]

Older students will enjoy the wit of Tom Lehrer's 'A Christmas Carol'. They will also appreciate the wit and truth of the following parody of the well-known Christian hymn 'All things bright and beautiful'.

All things dull and ugly
All creatures short and squat
All things rude and nasty
The Lord God made the lot

Each little snake that poisons
Each little wasp that stings
He made their prudish venom
He made their horrid wings

All things sick and cancerous
All evil great and small
All things foul and dangerous
The Lord God made them all.

Each nasty little hornet
Each beastly little squid
Who made the spikey urchin,
Who made the sharks? He did.

All things scabbed and ulcerous
All pox both great and small
Putrid, foul and gangrenous
The Lord God made them all.

Monty Python[20]

Students may also appreciate John Mole's 'Cat of Ages',[21] and 'Mystery', Doug MacLeod's parody of the film *Picnic at Hanging Rock*.[22]

Comic verse

The humour of comic verse is often quite outrageous, and its word play and ability to surprise us make it an attractive form. Most students respond positively to the following examples.

Somebody said that it couldn't be done –
But he with a grin, replied
He'd never been one to say it couldn't be done –
Leastways, not 'til he tried.
So he buckled right in, with a trace of a grin;
By golly, he went right to it.
He tackled the Thing That Couldn't Be Done!
And he couldn't do it.

Anon[23]

Car attack

On last year's Halloween
A car hit Aunty Jean.
Unhinged by this attack,
My Auntie hit it back.

She hit it with her handbag
And knocked it with her knee.
She socked it with a sandbag
And thumped it with a tree.

On last year's Halloween
A car hit Auntie Jean.
And now, my Auntie's better
But the car is with the wrecker.

Doug MacLeod[24]

Vegetarians

Vegetarians are cruel unthinking people.
Everybody knows that a carrot screams when grated
That a peach bleeds when torn apart.
Do you believe an orange insensitive
to thumbs gouging out its flesh?
That tomatoes spill their brains
painlessly? Potatoes, skinned alive
and boiled, the soil's little lobsters.
Don't tell me it doesn't hurt
when peas are ripped from their overcoats,
the hide flayed from sprouts,
cabbage shredded, onions beheaded.

Throw in the trowel and lay down the hoe.
Mow no more. Let my people go!

Roger McGough[25]

Nonsense poetry

Although nonsense poetry defies precise interpretation, one of its great exponents, Spike Milligan, describes it as "wreaking havoc with the English language and trying to puzzle the reader as much as you can".[26] Its special appeal and the key to its success with all age groups lie in its fantastic themes, absurd images, invented words and infectious rhythms.

Not all nonsense poetry, however, is humorous; some is stark and harsh and frightening such as Lewis Carroll's 'Jabberwocky' or sad such as his 'The Walrus and the Carpenter'. Indeed, when Tweedle Dum reads Alice this poem she responds with 'I know they're talking nonsense and it's foolish to cry about it' [the fate of the oysters] 'so she brushed away her tears'. Although there are some illustrated editions of 'Jabberwocky', I avoid them or only show them to students after they have read/heard the words and conjured up pictures of 'slithy toves', 'mome raths', 'Bandersnatch' and the 'Jabberwock' in their own minds. For a different perspective on 'Jabberwocky', read Doug MacLeod's poem 'Nonsense Rhyme', where he hypotheses that Lewis Carroll's inspiration came from an inebriated companion![27]

Other nonsense poetry such as Edward Lear's immortal 'The Owl and the Pussy Cat' (1871) is gentle, romantic and lyrical. I believe that every student should experience these masterpieces of nonsense poetry by Carroll and Lear.

The following poems, all of which can be found in *The Penguin Book of Nonsense Verse*,[28] provide a good introduction to nonsense poems:

- Lewis Carroll, 'Jabberwocky'
- Edward Lear, 'The Owl and The Pussycat'
- Hilaire Belloc, 'The Yak'
- Laura Richards, 'Eletelephony'
- Spike Milligan, 'On the Ning Nang Nong'
- Russell Hoban, 'Typo'.

The Walker Book of Poetry for Children[29] contains:

- Mervyn Peake, 'Sensitive, Seldom and Sad'
- Shel Silverstein, 'Jimmy Jet and His TV Set'
- Jack Prelutsky, 'Herbert Glerbert'.

Also worth reading to students are Charles Causley's 'Out in the Desert'[30] and Roald Dahl's 'The Crocodile'.[31]

Lyrical poetry

The term 'lyrical' is derived from a Greek word meaning 'for the lyre' (ie. meant to be sung), and lyrical poetry has retained a strong connection with singing and music since classical times. It is not concerned with action or narrative but rather with feeling. Usually representing or reflecting on a single experience, the modern lyric is intensely personal, and its rhythms often have a musical flexibility. Anne Bell's 'The Donkey' is a good example.

The Donkey

Her home is built of wind and sun,
Bird's song and butterfly's wings;
Roof of sky,
Carpet of grass
And the seasons hang their pictures on the wall.

Her eyes are wide and mild and kind,
Her muzzle soft as pussy-willow,
And her enormous ears hear things that we will never know
For sometimes
She thinks she remembers a dream,
Like sounds of singing, a stable, a child
And one great, glorious star.

Anne Bell[32]

Other beautiful lyrics by Anne Bell include *The little things*, *The caretaker* and *On rainy nights*.[33]

Some of my other favourites are:

Until I saw the Sea

Until I saw the sea
I did not know
that wind
could wrinkle water so.

I never knew
that sun
could splinter a whole sea of blue.

Nor
did I know before,
a sea breathes in and out
upon a shore.

Lilian Moore[34]

Watching Eye

In the corner of the garden
I noticed something lie
like a little chip of glass
so I gently stooped to pry.

A tiny spider watched me
with a tiny spider's eye.

Colin Thiele[35]

Narrative poetry

Since students of all ages enjoy a good story, teachers need to build on their love of picture books, easy 'chapter' books and novels with a range of stories in verse. Narrative poems with their strong story lines, memorable characters and vivid landscapes have a universal appeal. Also, the great diversity of themes in ballads, the short stanzas and the use of simple repetition, especially in the refrains, attract most readers. Students could even be encouraged to sing some of them.

The following narrative poems are 'oldies but goodies!', which can be found in most general anthologies and treasuries:

- Alfred Noyes, 'The Highwayman' (voted the 'best poem ever written' by a Year 6 class)
- Robert Browning, 'The Pied Piper of Hamelin'
- Samuel Taylor Coleridge, 'The Ancient Mariner'
- Henry Wadsworth Longfellow, 'Hiawatha'
- Alfred, Lord Tennyson, 'The Lady of Shalott'
- T.S. Eliot, 'Skimbleshanks: 'The Railway Cat'
- W.H. Auden, 'Nightmail'
- W.H. Auden, 'Miss Gee, a ballad'
- Charles Causley, 'Colonel Fazackerley'.

The following Australian bush ballads and story poems also fall into the category of narrative verse:[36]

- A.B. 'Banjo' Paterson, 'Clancy of the Overflow'
- A.B. 'Banjo' Paterson, 'The Man From Snowy River'
- A.B. 'Banjo' Paterson, 'The Man from Ironbark'
- A.B. 'Banjo' Paterson, 'Mulga Bill's Bicycle'
- Bill Scott, 'Lazy Jack'
- Thomas E. Spencer, 'How Macdougall Topped the Score'
- Anon, 'The Wild Colonial Boy' (which demands to be sung).

There are also illustrated paperback editions of *Clancy of the Overflow* and *The Man from Snowy River* but I would let the words speak for themselves. Illustrators give only their own interpretations! There are many other superb examples of modern Australian narratives, such as Max Fatchen's 'Children Lost'[37] that should not be missed.

Verse novels

The multi-layered verse novel is rapidly growing in popularity in Australia. Most are written in short chapters and free-verse lines and in the idiom of the young characters.

Some of Steven Herrick's verse novels have made their way onto prescribed reading lists in some states and have been regularly short-listed by The Children's Book Council of Australia. The following verse novels would be enjoyed by independent readers.

- Steven Herrick *The Spangled Drongo: A Verse Novel*[38]
- Steven Herrick *Tom Jones Saves the World*[39]
- Steven Herrick *Do Wrong Ron*[40]
- Susan Creech *Heartbeat*[41]
- Robert Cormier *Frenchtown Summer*[42]

Reading and Sharing Poetry

There is little doubt that reading poetry aloud is the best way for students to experience the joy and magic of the words, revel in the rhymes and rhythms and appreciate the themes. After all, most poetry was meant to be heard rather than read.

How and when to read poetry

- Make sure that students engage in poetry reading in a positive classroom environment. A suggestion is to bring the students physically close to you – on a carpet, bean bags or on chairs arranged in a circle.
- Make the reading environment a 'picture palace' of photographs, prints, poetry posters, friezes, models and mobiles, where the students can enjoy 'hanging around words'.
- To create atmosphere you could consider lowering the blinds or playing some appropriate background music.'
- It is vital that you practise before reading any poem out loud, heeding the advice of D.H. Lawrence that "it all depends on the *pause* – the *natural lingering* pause, the natural lingering of the voice according to the feeling – it is the hidden emotional pattern that makes poetry, not its obvious form".[43]
- Make reading poetry out loud a regular daily feature of your teaching program.
- Encourage students to read poetry in 'drop everything and read' periods.
- Read poems in breaks between lessons and the beginning and end of the day. Before going out to recess or lunch read an 'I'm hungry' poem. Read a 'windy' or 'rainy' poem to reflect the weather of the day and poems to celebrate special events such as birthdays, Anzac Day and Harmony Day.
- Since many poems are not easy to grasp at the first reading, follow up with repeated readings. A second (or third) reading of memorable poetry usually enhances enjoyment and increases understanding. As Walter de la Mare said,

"at every reading of a poem, though it may have been familiar since early childhood, some hitherto hidden delicacy of rhythm or intonation may be revealed".[44]

- Learn a poem 'off by heart' and recite it from memory. Students find this a mesmerising experience and many adults attribute their continuing love affair with poetry directly to having heard an impassioned teacher perform in this way.

- Have students choose a 'poem for the week' and, after practising, read it aloud to the class. If many are humorous poems, you could have a class discussion on how the language, theme, rhyme creates the humour.

- Invite a poet to read his/her poems to the students. In some states, funding is available to help disadvantaged children meet and work with children's writers and illustrators. The National Literacy and Numeracy Week also gives awards to schools that encourage literacy through innovative programs: look at their website at <www.literacyandnumeracy.gov.au>.

- Let the students hear other voices. Invite the Principal, a parent, a footballer, a senior citizen or the local bank manager to read a poem to the class.

- Instead of reading a story in prose, read a chapter of a verse novel each day.

- Create a mood for thematic poetry 'studies'. When reading poems about pets, photographs of the students' own pets can be displayed, along with pet poem posters, mobiles in pet shapes. Perhaps the students can bring their pets to class. Although you may wish to restrict these to birds, goldfish, guinea pigs, rabbits, I once saw a cat strolling nonchalantly around the classroom during the reading of a selection of T.S. Eliot's cat poems.

Because students tend to regard poems in books and on printed sheets as something greater than one of their own poems, you could use Rex Rehn's suggestion of handwriting poems in coloured pens onto overhead projector transparencies and showing them to the class.[45]

Responding to Poetry

The first thing to remember is that taste in poetry, like all the arts, is a very personal matter. Readers will, therefore, respond to poems in widely different ways. Some laugh out loud, some cry, some shudder, some yawn, some come out in goose bumps and some respond with a period of contemplative silence. "The problem for teachers is how to move from the original felt response to a more critical response without destroying the initial delight and without imposing their own viewpoint."[46]

While English syllabus documents have long called for honest and thoughtful responses to poetry rather than responses based on information about figurative language, rhyming schemes and metre, it is often difficult to convince well-intentioned teachers to trust their own personal judgements. This is not to say that students should not be introduced to poetic techniques but this should always take place when needed and in context.

You should build on students' first responses with a range of talking, listening and writing activities which, if imaginative and relevant, will expand and refine the initial reaction and produce a more considered response. Remember:

- to accept and respect every student's response – there are as many interpretations of a poem as there are readers;
- to recognise/ affirm that it is quite legitimate not to like a particular poem. Many students believe that because the teacher chose the poem it must be good. Many may well be 'miserable' choices;
- to share a poem that you do not like. I use Elizabeth Honey's 'Looking after Granny', which most students find hilarious. When I ask why they think I do not like it, they invariably suggest 'because you're a granny' or 'because you're very old'. Since they are partially correct I agree;
- to reinforce/ affirm that poetry is not a code to be cracked nor a clock to be fixed. Deciphering a code or dismantling a clock is unlikely to help understand what it means. Judith Wright once observed that:

  It looks rather odd to a poet to see whole shoals of students who neither want to write poetry nor to know how it was written, being solemnly taught how to take a poem to pieces, but all too seldom how to put it together again, or what to do with it in order to enjoy it;[47]

- to recognise that meaning may differ from reader to reader, depending on individual experience and sensibility to what is being said;
- not to destroy the beauty, wonder and delight by seeking to interpret each word. Although poets may be the original masters of the words, the readers are the ones who make the meaning (and words can mean so many things);
- to ask the students if there are any words that they do not understand after the reading. However, do not assume that students will not know the meaning as a narrow dictionary meaning may not be the one intended. Readers do not have to understand every word to enjoy the poetic experience. I have never had to explain the meaning of words such as 'talons', 'fangs' or 'dismember' when reading Jack Prelutsky's 'A Dragon's Lament' because I demonstrate their meaning through gestures and/or facial expressions;
- to avoid comprehension exercises like the plague! They have, generally, had a deplorable effect on the teaching of poetry;
- to focus on enjoyment and let understanding come in its own good time.

Response through talking and listening activities

There are several ways to ensure that talking and listening activities are productive and enjoyable for the whole class.

- Make a regular time (a 'read and tell' session) to share the poems that students have added to their personal anthologies (see Chapter 3). Discuss why they chose particular poems.

- Provide time for students to talk about their responses in pairs or in small groups.

- Direct and structure the informal talk by providing some questions. Aidan Chambers's framework of 'Tell me' questions[48] is an excellent resource which, used wisely, will move students from talking about likes and dislikes to talking about things that puzzled them and to finding satisfying patterns inside the text.

- Have the students find a poem (preferably not too short) with which you are unfamiliar. Model an oral response. Let the students see you 'musing and puzzling' over meaning, which will not only reinforce an atmosphere of openness in the classroom but will also make students feel more confident about their own responses.

- Use Penny Blackie's technique to create a discussion base. To avoid a teacher-led agenda, she asked students to jot down their responses to the poem while reading it, such as a line they liked or an image or a word or a general reaction to the poem. Students could write anything as long as it was written as a question (for example, an initial reponse of 'Felt sad' becomes 'Why did I feel sad when I read this poem?'; 'Funny description of aunty' becomes 'Why is the description of the aunty funny?'). The questions were then collected and became the basis for devising the lesson.[49]

- Suggest that students record their responses to a particular poem on tape at home or at school. Ask them to record their first response and then, after several re-readings of the poem, return to it a week later. Students may respond differently over time as fresh insights are gained. After all, response to any literary stimulus is "more like a negative in a developing dish than a train coming through a tunnel".[50]

- Have different students or teachers prepare and read the same poem. Ask your class to reflect on how the readers use emphasis, intonation and pause to create different interpretations.

- Have the students listen to well-known poets performing their own work on tape, such as the following:
  - Steven Herrick *Poetry to the Rescue and More*[51]
  - Steven Herrick *Tom Jones Saves the World*[52]
  - Jack Prelutsky *The Frog Wore Red Suspenders*[53]
  - Spike Milligan *Spike's Poems*.[54]

Response through writing activities

Try some of the following activities for getting students to write about poetry and their responses to poems.

- Have students keep a 'poetry journal' in which they write their personal responses to poems that they have either heard read aloud in class or 'found' in anthologies. For a fascinating introduction to this approach, read Sharon Creech's *Love That Dog*. The interaction of the teacher, Miss Stretchberry, and a young boy (unnamed) cleverly illustrates the effect of poetry on a group of students. Miss Stretchberry introduces a number of different poems to her class, encouraging the students to respond in their diaries, and eventually to write their own poems. The young boy's responses to some of the American 'classic' poets, such as Robert Frost, are absolutely delightful. After listening to the poem 'Stopping by woods on a snowy evening', he writes:

What was up with
The snowy woods poem
You read today?

Why doesn't the person just keep going if he's got
So many miles to go before he sleeps?

When the teacher reads another Robert Frost poem, 'The Pasture', he responds (having already decided 'that any words can be a poem. You've just got to make short lines') with the following comment:

I think Mr. Robert Frost
has a little
too
much time
on his
hands.[55]

- Ask students to create their own poetry anthologies. Some teachers use this activity to develop handwriting skills. Alternatively, when students type their entries, it is a marvellous way for them to focus on poetic form and language, which indirectly improves their own writing skills. They will quickly notice that the computer automatically inserts capital letters at the beginning of each line and will question punctuation and spelling. Invented spellings in the poem throw up some interesting substitutes from the word-processing thesaurus!

- In a lesson focused on reading you can give students a direction with some instructions such as those suggested by Andrew Stibbs: "… I want you to have made a note of the title and sources of three poems; one which you want to copy out and keep, one you wish to read aloud to us next lesson and one which you think the rest of the class might enjoy and discuss".[56]

- Ask students to write their instant reactions to a poem and then share these with a partner who, in turn, is asked to respond in writing.
- In Chapters 5 and 6 there are suggestions on how students can write their own poems. They can take one they have read to use as a model or to parody, or they can write an original poem.

Other ways to respond to poetry

- Have students draw their response or create a doodle or pattern.
- Have them use paints or coloured pencils to reflect the mood of the poem. Just put a colour in a column headed 'happy,' 'sad' or 'angry'.
- Supply each student with a set of cards numbered from 1 to 10 and let them 'score' a poem which has been read aloud. Have the students who gave the poem a '1' sit with those who marked it '10' and compare the reasons for their responses.

The Language of Poetry

It is vital that students respond first to the poet's words before focusing on his/her craft. However, it may be necessary at some stage to introduce a few of the techniques and technical devices that poets use. Always look at these techniques within the context of the entire poem to see the poet's purpose in using them.

Rhythm

Not all poets use rhyme or figurative language but **all** poets use rhythm and sound which they believe are the heart of the poem. Rhythm is as natural as breathing, as regular as your heartbeat, the pulse of your blood and the ebb and flow of tides.

Rather than talking about metre and stressed and unstressed syllables in a poem, let students experience rhythm by reading them poems with very strong rhythms. Show them how that rhythm projects the mood and action of the poem. The tempo and driving speed of trains can be easily heard in Robert Louis Stevenson's 'From a Railway Carriage', W.H. Auden's 'Night Mail' and Libby Hathorn's 'There and Back'[57] just as the pounding gallop is appreciated in Robert Louis Stevenson's 'Windy Nights'. Ask students to find poems about horses or wind or sea and read them aloud to experience the rhythm. After reading these poems, you can discuss how the poet used repetition, assonance and alliteration to develop a particular rhythm.

You can also demonstrate how the rhythm of everyday speech works in modern poems, such as those written by Michael Rosen and Steven Herrick. Sometimes this rhythm does not quite work. When I read one of my favourite poems written in free verse, I always leave out one line because I find it jarring – and the omission does not affect the impact of the poem. Recently, when I admitted to the poet that I did this, he replied 'I know – it doesn't scan'.

Rhyme

This is the device that children are probably most familiar with. It involves the repetition of the final sound of a word, from a stressed syllable onwards, and is most commonly found at the end of lines – eg. *free/sea* in the second and fourth lines of this stanza from Coleridge's 'Rime of the Ancient Mariner':

> *The fair breeze blew, the white foam flew,*
> *The furrow followed free;*
> *We were the first that ever burst*
> *Into that silent sea.*

However, this stanza is unusual in that it also contains internal rhymes (*blew/flew* and *first/burst*) in the first and third lines. All these rhymes involve only one stressed syllable and are called 'masculine'; rhymes involving more than one syllable (eg. *cable/table*) are called 'feminine'.

Rhyme pulls words together and makes them comment on each other. Rhyme is extremely difficult to do well but, says Gerard Benson, when well done it enriches the meanings of words and works like a kind of magic.[58] Some poets like Jack Prelutsky use it with skill and imagination. So too does James Reeves, as in 'W'.

> *The King sent for his wise men all*
>   *To find a rhyme for W.*
> *When they had thought a good long time*
> *But could not think of a single rhyme,*
> *'I'm sorry,' said he, 'to trouble you.'*

James Reeves[59]

I thoroughly recommend Gerard Benson's *Does W Trouble You?* – its introduction in the form of letters to the editor provides students with very real insights to the way rhyme works or does not! Although understanding how rhyming schemes are used in poems does not add to the enjoyment of the genre, I have found many students actually like the game of finding the pattern (*aa, bb,* or *ab, ab,* etc.) and quickly comment that the rhyming is 'regular', it makes the poem 'funny', and even that the use of internal rhyme is 'clever and effective'.

Onomatopoeia

What a frabjous word! Simply, it means the coining or use of words that imitate the sound of the thing. To illustrate this poetic device, use the following strategy. Ask the students to put their heads on the desk and close their eyes. Ask them to listen carefully to any sounds that they hear. After a few minutes, ask them what they heard and write their responses on the blackboard. One class in an inner-city school heard the noises of traffic, footsteps in the corridor and children in the local pre-school. When asked to describe the sounds they offered 'screeching' (brakes on a car) 'hooting' and 'honking' (car horns), 'squealing' (young children playing) 'thudding' (footsteps in the corridor). Then tell them that when words imitate the sound of things we call that onomatopoeia (broken down on the board to ono/mato/poeia). Finally, read them the following poems to illustrate this poetic device.

A Swamp Romp

Clomp Thump
Swamp Lump
Plodding in the Ooze,
Belly shiver
Jelly quiver
Squelching in my shoes.

Clomp Thump
Romp Jump
Mulching all the Mud,
Boot Trudge
Foot Sludge
Thud! Thud! Thud !

Doug MacLeod[60]

Breakdown

Rackerty clackerty
Clackerty BONG
The washing machine has gone
   terribly wrong.

Jean Kenward[61]

Our Washing Machine

Our washing machine went whisity whirr
Whisity, whisity, whirr.
One day at noon it went whisity click!
Whisity, whisity, whisity click!
Click, **grr**, click, **grr**, click, **grr**, click!
Call the repairman.
Fix it … Quick!

Patricia Hubbell[62]

Some poets particularly relish the challenge of orchestrating the sound of their verse in this imitative way; here is a virtuoso display by Tennyson from 'Morte d'Arthur', describing Sir Bedivere carrying his mortally wounded king:

The bare black cliff clang'd round him, as he based
His feet on juts of slippery crag that rang
Sharp-smitten with the dint of armed heels –
And on a sudden, lo! the level lake,
And the long glories of the winter moon.

The contrast between the perils of the journey and the smooth prospect of the lake, the king's final destination, is conveyed in the sound and movement of the verse with wonderful skill. Note how alliteration and assonance both play important parts in the total effect.

Alliteration

Alliteration is the echo of consonantal sounds in several words placed close together, as in this anonymous line:

Swarthy smoke-blackened smiths, smudged with soot.

Usually the echoing consonants occur at the beginning of the words, as with the 's' sounds here and the 'f' sounds in the first two lines of Coleridge's stanza quoted above, but they can also occur elsewhere in a word. Alliteration is called 'partial' when not all the consonants are repeated (eg. *silver stars*).

Assonance

Assonance involves the echoing of vowel sounds rather than consonants and so is closely related to rhyme. The first line of one of Shakespeare's songs from *The Tempest* is held together partly by the assonance of three long 'i' sounds:

Full fathom five thy father lies …

Poets use assonance and alliteration, sometimes in combination (as here), to make patterns of sound and meaning. These patterns reinforce each other, forming extra connections within the texture of the verse.

Similarities and differences – metaphor, simile and personification

A **metaphor** implies a relationship in which similarity or difference is a significant feature. A metaphor draws attention to resemblances between two things, but instead of using 'like' or 'as', it boldly states (or assumes) that one thing is another:

The sea is a hungry dog
Giant and grey.

This is the beginning of 'The Sea' by James Reeves,[63] and the metaphor of the 'giant sea-dog' is sustained for the whole length of the poem. But a metaphor can also be condensed into a single phrase, as in the second half of this line from Alfred Noyes' 'The Highwayman':

His rapier hilt a-twinkle under the jewelled sky.

While some poets use metaphors that are merely decorative or illustrative, skilful poets use it to change our perceptions, feelings and thoughts. Used well, it is a powerful poetic tool. By stating that one thing is another, it forces the reader into another imaginative world. So, the sea becomes a 'hungry dog', or 'a battering ram' and balloons become 'wild space animals'. Often established in the first line of the poem, the poet will then sustain the metaphor through the use of say 'dog' words or 'animal' words, with the result that the entire poem is an extended metaphor. F. R. McCreary's 'The Fog' (see Chapter 3) is a fine example of extended metaphor.

Metaphors may provide real challenges for students who, having been exposed to a lot of factual writing, often reject the comparison! Just for fun, you might like to read Steven Herrick's 'A Metaphor Poem'. The following is an extract:

A Metaphor Poem

Our teacher Ms Stevrakis
Wanted us to read a metaphor poem.
Sam asked, "What is a meta for?"
But Sarah saved the day
By raising her hand and
Saying that a metaphor is when you say
  "Sam is a goat".
Tomorrow,
Ms Stevrakis is going to teach us onomatopoeia.
Sam said that if you put a mat on a pier
  It would get wet.

Steven Herrick[64]

All students are familiar with **similes**. They use them in their everyday speech and are surrounded by them in their media environment. This device involves comparing one thing with another using either 'like' or 'as'.

An emerald is as green as grass:
A ruby red as blood:
A sapphire shines as blue as heaven . . .

Christina Rossetti[65]

Rather than have students pick out a simile from a given poem, send them off on a 'simile' hunt. Have some unusual, outrageous and stimulating examples planted around the classroom or playground – along with some red herrings – and give a prize for the one who collects the most.

Personification is the presentation of an object or idea as a person or with human qualities or feelings. The opening of James Stephens' short poem 'The Wind' shows its potential:

The wind stood up and gave a shout;
He whistled on his fingers, and
Kicked the withered leaves about,
And thumped the branches with his hand.[66]

Many students will have already encountered this device in nursery rhymes and other poems. They will also be able to tell you that their dog 'laughs'. Draw their attention to the fact that many metaphors embrace personification. Have students personify objects in the classroom – let their imaginations run wild! Display their responses on a wall poster and ask them to vote for their favourite.

Symbolism is a term used to refer to poetry in which a word or image signifies something other than what it literally denotes, so that it carries enlarging connotations.

Symbols tend to stand for abstractions and may be regarded as metaphors with a rich but indefinite suggestiveness. The sun is often used as a symbol for light, warmth and clarity; the moon in all its phases for beauty, magic, mystery and change. Colours are frequently used as symbols too: for instance, red for passion and blood; white for purity, innocence and beauty.

Imagery is a term that is sometimes used to mean figurative language. However, imagery, which involves vivid description, does not necessarily have to include figures of speech. An image can be effectively conveyed by the choice and order of the words, as shown in the first stanza of Lilian Moore's 'Until I Saw the Sea':

Until I saw the sea
I did not know
that wind
could wrinkle water so.[67]

References

1   Auden, WH (1953) Introduction to de la Mare, W *Come Hither: A Collection of Rhymes and Poems for the Young of all Ages*. Faber p3.

2   Mitchell, A (ed.) (1996) *The Orchard Book of Poems*. Orchard Books p14.

3   Causley, C (1985) 'Inside Poetry: A Shared Adventure' in McVitty, W (ed.) *Word Magic: Poetry as a Shared Adventure*. PETA, Sydney p9.

4   White, E B (1973) 'On writing for children', in Haviland, V (ed.), *Children and Literature: Views and Reviews*. Scott, Foresman & Co., Glenview, IL p140.

5   Fox, G et al (1976) 'A Defence of Rubbish' in *Writers Critics and Children*. Agathon Press p75.

6   Morrow, R and King, S M (1996) *Beetle Soup*. Scholastic.

7   Thiele, C (2003) *Sun warm memories: The Colin Thiele Reciter*. Triple D Books.

8   Haviland, V (ed.) (1973) 'Mother Goose's Garnishings' in *Children and Literature. Views and Reviews*. Scott, Foresman & Co. p190.

9   Fatchen, M (1999) *Songs for My Dog and Other Wry Rhymes*. Wakefield Press. Reprinted with the kind permission of the poet.

10 *ibid*. Reprinted with permission.

11 Dugan, M and MacLeod, D (1993) *Out to Lunch*. Moondrake.

12 McNaughton, C (1987) *There's an awful lot of weirdos in our neighbourhood*. Walker Books.

13 Tulloch, R (1999) *Mixy's Mixed-up Rhymes*. ABC Books.

14 *Mad* magazine 1976. EC Publications Inc.

15 McGough, R (ed.) (1991) *The Kingfisher Book of Comic Verse*. Kingfisher.

16 Foster, J (ed) Mackie, C & Stevens, T (ills.) (2003) *101 Favourite Poems*. Collins, London.

17 Blake, Q (1996) *The Penguin Book of Nonsense Verse*. Puffin Poetry

18 Honey, E (1998) *Mongrel Doggerel*. Allen & Unwin. Reprinted with the kind permission of the poet.

19 Agard, J & Nichols, G (eds.) (2004) *From Mouth to Mouth: Oral Poems from Around the World*. Walker Books.

20 *Monty Python's Life of Brian*. Methuen, London.

21 Mole, J (1994) *Back By Midnight*. Puffin.

22 MacLeod, D (2004) *Spiky, Spunky, My Pet Monkey*. Puffin.

23 Prelutsky, J (ed.) (1994) *For Laughing Out Loud: Poems to Tickle Your Funnybone*. Red Fox.

24 MacLeod, D (1981) *In the Garden of Badthings*. Kestrel/Picture Puffin. Reprinted with the kind permission of the poet.

25 'Vegetarians' by Roger McGough from *Holiday on Death Row* (© Roger McGough 1979) is reproduced by permission of PFD (www.pfd.co.uk) on behalf of Roger McGough.

26 Milligan, S (1989) *Startling Verse for all the Family*. Puffin Books.

27 MacLeod, D (2004) *op.cit.*

28 Blake, Q *op.cit.*

29 Prelutsky, J (ed.) & Lobel, A (ill.) (1985) *The Walker Book of Poetry for Children*. Walker Books, London.

30 Causley, C & Payne, L (ill.) (1994) *Going to the Fair – Selected poems for Children*. Puffin Books.

31 Dahl, R & Blake, Q (ill.) (1986) *Dirty Beasts*. Puffin Books.

32 Scott-Mitchell, C & Griffith, K (eds.) (2002) *100 Australian poems for children*. Random House, Australia. Reprinted with the kind permission of the poet.

33   all in Morrow, R and King, S M *op.cit.*

34   Moore, L (1967) *I Feel the Same Way.* Atheneum.

35   Morrow, R and King, S M *op.cit.* Reprinted with the kind permission of the poet.

36   all in Robinson, M (ed.) & Smith, C (ill.) (1999) *Waltzing Matilda meets Lazy Jack.* Silverfish.

37   Fatchen, M (1987) *A Paddock of Poems.* Penguin Books, Australia.

38   Herrick, S (1999) *The Spangled Drongo.* UQP.

39   Herrick, S (2002) *Tom Jones Saves The World.* UQP.

40   Herrick, S (2002) *Do-Wrong Ron.* Allen & Unwin.

41   Creech, S (2004) *Heartbeat.* Bloomsbury.

42   Cormier, R (2000) *Frenchtown Summer.* Puffin Books.

43   Allen, J & Angelotti, M (1982) 'Responding to Poetry'. *New Essays in the Teaching of Literature. Proceedings of the Literature Commission Third Internationl Conference on the Teaching of English, Sydney Australia 1980.* Australian Association of Teaching English p168.

44   McVitty, W (ed.) (1985) *Word Magic: Poetry as a Shared Adventure.* PETA, Sydney p4.

45   Rehn, R (1992) 'Reading and Writing Poetry' in Thomson, J (ed.) *Reconstructing Literature Teaching.* AATE, Adelaide p119.

46   Watson, K (1981) *English Teaching in Perspective.* St Clair Press, Sydney.

47   Wright, J (1966) 'The Role of Poetry in Education'. *English in Australia;* June:2.

48   Chambers, A (1994) *Tell Me: Children, Reading and Talk.* PETA in association with Thimble Press, Sydney pp83-92.

49   Blackie, P (1971) 'Asking questions'. *English in Education;* 5: 3 p23.

50   Britton, J (1983) 'Reading and writing poetry' in Arnold, R (ed.) *Timely Voices: English Teaching in the Eighties.* Oxford University Press, Melbourne p11.

51   Herrick, S (2002) *Poetry to the Rescue and More.* Vocal Eyes.

52   Herrick, S (2003) *Tom Jones Saves the World.* Vocal Eyes.

53   Prelutsky, J (2002) *The Frog Wore Red Suspenders.* Harper Children's Audio.

54   Milligan, S (2002) *Spike's Poems.* ABC Radio Collection.

55   Creech, S (2001) *Love That Dog.* Bloomsbury. Reprinted courtesy Bloomsbury Publishing.

56   Stibbs, A (1981) 'Poetry in the classroom', *Children's Literature in Education:*40 p47.

57   all in Morrow, R and King, S M *op.cit.*

58   Benson, G (1995) *Does W Trouble You?* Puffin Books p11.

59   Reeves, J *The Complete Poems for Children.* Heinemann. Reprinted courtesy Laura Cecil Literary Agency.

60   MacLeod, D (1981) *op.cit.* Reprinted with the kind permission of the poet.

61   Rumble, A (ed.) (1989) *Is A Caterpillar Ticklish?* Puffin Books.

62   Hubbell, P. *The Apple Vendor's Fair.* Atheneum Publishers.

63   Reeves, J *op.cit.*

64   Herrick, S (1997) *My Life, My Love, My Lasagne.* UQP. Reprinted with the kind permission of the poet.

65   Prelutsky, J & Lobel, A *op.cit.*

66   Stephens, J 1882-1950.

67   Moore, L *op.cit.*

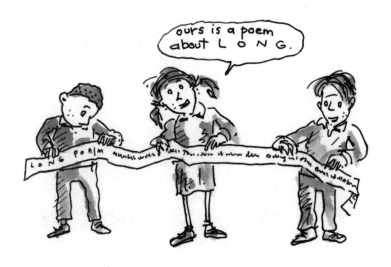

3

Classroom Activities for Enjoying Poetry

The following activities have been designed not only to increase enjoyment of poetry but also to make poetry more accessible to students, developing their appreciation of the genre. Teachers will need to refine, modify and develop these ideas to meet the needs and interests of their own classes. I have not suggested specific age groups for each activity as I have found that even very young students have an amazing ability to surprise you with their insights, imagination and abilities. Finally, as Geoff Fox and Brian Merrick remind us, "Any classroom activity in teaching a poem should bring reader and text closer together, not come between them."[1]

Compiling Anthologies

Different anthologies can be developed for different purposes and audiences.

Personal anthologies

Students can compile personal anthologies of their favourite poems. Try to encourage them to select from different poetic forms and include poems they have written themselves. They may like to add a comment as to why they chose a particular poem along the lines of 'I like this poem because …'. They may also like to illustrate their anthology.

Class anthologies

These poems can be randomly selected from class favourites or can be focused on a theme, such as school, families, food, animals. However, the problem in using themes is that it is often tempting to choose a poem simply because it is connected with the theme, without considering its merits as a poem. You may need to monitor the inclusions.

Anthologies for different audiences

Students can prepare anthologies for different audiences, such as a kindergarten class, children in hospital or senior citizens in a retirement village. This activity makes students consider:

- the importance of the audience;
- the suitability of theme, form and language;
- the impact of accompanying illustrations.

Arrange for students to read or perform poems from their anthologies to their selected audience and reflect on whether their selections were appropriate.

Poetry Surveys

Have your students design a questionnaire to find out how people of various ages, cultures and occupations view poetry. Respondents could be students' parents or siblings, school peers, students from other classes or schools, or community groups. Some questions which might be posed:

- Do you like poetry? Why? Why not?
- What makes poetry different from other kinds of writing?
- What subjects do you think poets usually write about?
- Have you got a favourite poem? If 'yes' the interviewee may like to recite it and to offer an opinion as to why they remember it. (Hopefully, some may respond with 'an inspirational teacher'!)
- Where did you first hear or read it?
- Do you think poetry should be taught in schools?

This activity provides a good lead-in to a class discussion on attitudes to poetry, and to the following activity.

Marketing Poetry

Conduct a campaign to 'sell' poetry to the uncommitted and unconvinced. Students can design handbills, advertisements, badges, slogans and T-shirts. Steven Herrick's poem 'Advertisements for poetry' is a good starting point.

Advertisements for Poetry

Buy Poetry.
New improved formula.
Chocolate-coated poetry.
A glass and a half of full-cream rhyme in every poem.
The taste that refreshes, drink poetry.
Poetry, don't leave home without it.
A poem a day helps you work rest and play.
Always poetry.
Ready for a change, try poetry.
Life would be pretty straight without poetry.
Take two poems and see your doctor if pain persists.
Start your day with a bowl of Special P
(for poetry).
No added sugar, artificial flavours or colours.
Everyone around the world keeps singing McPoetry.
It won't happen overnight but it will happen
        With poetry.
Lose 10 kilos in 5 weeks with low-fat poetry.
Poetry – it works for me, it could work for you too!
Try Poetry, today.

Note: Poetry should not be taken by people afraid to laugh,
              or those on a poetry-free diet. Nine out of ten doctors
              recommend poetry for a longer life.

Steven Herrick[2]

Students could also prepare video clips, audio 'grabs' and select or write some background music.

This activity appeals to students and involves them in critically examining exposition texts and the language of persuasion. It also combines several curriculum areas, such as Creative Arts, Studies of Society and Environment, Information and Communication Technologies (even Mathematics when discussing demographics and circulation statistics). If they are encouraged to write advertisements for ethnic radio stations, newspapers and magazines, students from non-English speaking backgrounds will be able to incorporate language and music from their country of origin.

Reworking Poems

Cloze

Cloze activities involve deleting certain words from a text and having students speculate about possibilities for filling the gaps. Although some critics dislike cloze activities and dismiss them as mere guessing games, they can be an excellent way to introduce a poem and, by having students speculate on possible word choices, compel them to focus not only on rhyme and metre but also on meaning, syntax and register.

It is important to select a poem where the poet has used unusual words, ideas and images. In order to elicit meaningful responses, leave the first two or three lines intact. Many years ago, I was introduced to Judith Thurman's 'Balloons' by Vivienne Nicoll-Hatton and I have since used it with primary, secondary and tertiary students and have found that it works well (albeit differently) at each level.

Cloze activity

Balloons!

A balloon
is a wild
space animal,

restless pet
who bumps and _____
its head
on the cage walls
of a room

bursts
with a _____
or escapes slowly
with sighs
leaving a _____ skin.

Balloons
On the street

_____
in fresh air,
strain
at their string _____

If you loose
a balloon,
it _____ home
for the moon.

Judith Thurman[3]

The words chosen by the poet were 'butts', 'bellow', 'limp', 'fidget', 'leashes', 'bolts'.

TEACHING STEPS

- Have students work in pairs. Suggest that rather than putting in the first word they think of, they should make a list of possible words and select which one(s) they think are most appropriate, interesting or surprising. Invented words are acceptable!

- When the students have completed 'their' poem, make a blackboard summary of their choices.
- Have a class discussion about the choices. Which ones do they like/dislike? Why did they choose particular ones?

  It is worth noting that most students will opt for a verb for the first omission, a noun for the second, an adjective for the third. Draw their attention to this with comments (depending on their age and level of ability) such as 'What a wonderful choice of verbs' or 'I love your verb'. Older students will say they chose a word that rhymed or which expressed a similar sound, or a word or letter which they repeated for effect, so this is an opportunity to have a brief discussion about poetic devices.

- Then reveal the poet's words on an overhead transparency. It is important in this exercise to reveal only one missing word at a time. This could lead to some discussion as to why the poet chose these words, how they support the word pictures she was trying to create, whether students agree with her and whether they think any of the words they chose are more effective.

- When the whole poem is completed, most students will see that they have used 'balloon' words, whereas the poet has used 'animal' words. Remind them of the first stanza in which she states that they are 'space animals'. Discuss the effectiveness of her imaginative description. Some will argue that some of her words such as 'limp' are 'weak' and do not have the same impact as others such as 'bellow'. Remind students that it is not the number of words a poem uses but the force of the words and the range and depth of the images they evoke that is important.

- Have the students read out their completed poems. They will soon hear that certain words do not 'fit' (scan) and that those words disturb the rhythm of the poem.

- Have a class discussion based on the following questions:
  – What is the poet trying to say?
  – How does she say it?
  – Is she successful?

  Remember every response is personal and it is quite acceptable to not like a particular poem.

Other cloze activities

Students can attempt another cloze activity. You might like to try James Reeves's 'The Sea'[4] in which he compares the sea to a 'hungry dog'. Ask students to look for 'dog' words rather than 'sea' words. The poem is a useful lead-in to writing metaphor poems (see Chapter 5).

Alternative to cloze

Mike Hayhoe admits to "not being impressed by cloze procedures" and offers an alternative which he believes gives students time to "dwell with a poem and to use their feeling intellect as they decide upon which word to use". He suggests that teachers write out a short poem with options at various points and, although recognising that Thomas Hardy's 'I look into my glass' may not be ideal to start with, he provides the first stanza of this poem as an example for this activity.[5]

I _____ into my glass,
And _____ my wasting skin,
And ____, 'Would God it came to pass
My heart had _____ as thin!'

Thomas Hardy[6]

The words chosen by Hardy were 'look', 'view', 'say' 'shrunk'.

'Disturbed' poems

Another way of having students examine word choices is to use a 'disturbed' poem, in which the words have been altered rather than deleted. In this activity you alter words that carry the poem's meaning (especially imagery) or draw attention to the poem's form. It is important to give the students some clues, such as how many words are affected or which lines have been changed. Here is a 'disturbed' version of F.R. McCreary's 'The Fog' as an example.

'Disturbed' poem activity

The Fog

Slowly, the fog,
Hunch-shouldered with a pink face,
Arms wide, advances,
Finger tips scratching the way
Past the dark houses
And dark gardens of roses.
Up the short street from the harbour,
Slowly, the fog,
Seeking, seeking;
Arms wide, shoulders squared,
Looking, searching.
Out through the streets to the fields,
Slowly, the fog –
A deaf man hunting the sun.

F.R. McCreary[7]

There are six substitutions here: 'pink' for 'grey', 'scratching' for 'touching', 'squared' for 'hunched', 'Looking' for 'Searching' and, in the final line, 'deaf' for 'blind' and 'sun' for 'moon'. All of them bear in some way or other on the central image of the fog as a blind man.

Patterning Poetry

Poetry is usually clearly patterned in print or sound and some poems are enhanced by the poet's deliberate visual patterning of the words on the page. The following activity leads students to an appreciation of the different ways that poets physically shape their texts. This practical activity allows students to play with patterning or the siting of words on a page.

When writing free verse, poets work very carefully on composition such as punctuation and line breaks. Mary Manning and Jennifer O'Neill[8] have designed an activity that allows students to experiment with different ways of using lines in poetry. They suggest that, after writing several drafts of their poems, students can use a word processor to experiment with various structures. Students can see how their poem(s) will look when they:

- centre the whole poem;
- align the poem to the right;
- start each line with a capital letter;
- omit all capital letters;
- add punctuation;
- delete all punctuation;
- use more or fewer stanza breaks or stanzas with uneven numbers of lines; or
- add an extra space between lines where there is an obvious change in tone or situation.

Students then print out the version that they like best and discuss the effects of different formatting on the meaning or mood of the poem.

Re-siting a poem

To illustrate the work (or play) drafts of his poems, Robert Graves wrote two versions of his poem, 'Poem: a Reminder'. The first is a conventional set of six rhyming lines. Each line starts with a capital letter, the lines are centred on the page and there are gaps between the verses. The last two lines read:

To mean: 'Read carefully. Each word we chose
Has rhythm and sound and sense. This is not prose.'

In his second version, he re-sites the poem so that those two lines appear as:

...to mean read

care
-fully each word we chose has

rhythm and
sound and
sense this is

not prose.[9]

Mike Hayhoe uses this example to demonstrate how poets play around with layouts. He suggests dividing the class into small groups where students choose a poem and re-site its words upon a page. This activity allows them to become more aware of the power of the original and how the siting can in itself intensify the meaning of a poem.[10]

Using a different genre

In the previous activity Robert Graves reminds his readers that poetry is 'not prose'. Having students re-work a poem into a piece of prose (eg. newspaper article, letter, report etc.) is a useful activity that allows them to reflect on the differences. As a class, they can discuss what has been gained or lost in the re-working.

Text Reconstruction

This activity is an interesting way of exploring the structure of a poem and a way for students to see into a particular poet's mind. Recently, when using this exercise with students, one group decided to omit two lines from the given poem because, as they said, 'they just weren't right'. On reflection, I think they had a point!

Teaching steps

- Cut a number of poems into lines or stanzas and place them in envelopes. A word of warning – these need to be cut with a guillotine so that the lines are uniformly straight, otherwise wily students will put the poem together using the paper cuts rather than the words!

- Choose poems of varying degrees of difficulty (rhyming poems for young students and free verse for older or more capable students) and select a variety of themes and poetic forms.
- Have students in pairs or small groups put the poem together by placing the words in what they believe is the best order.
- Present them with the original poem and discuss the poet's imaginative use of language. Are their poems better? Why/Why not?

Extension activities

- **Poem reconstruction file:** Prepare a whole host of cut-up texts (keeping each poem together) and place them in a file in the classroom. Students who have finished a task (in any subject) can opt to 'do' a poem reconstruction. Make sure you have copies of the original for them to check.
- **Collage:** Ask students to cut out headlines, words, advertisements and photographs from newspapers and magazines. Students can arrange these on a page to form a 'poem'. The results can be sheer nonsense or deeply serious.

Missing Titles

This activity involves presenting a poem to a class – minus its title. Students then read the poem very carefully, look for clues and propose a title.

Teaching steps

- Select poems where the title is not obvious.
- Read each poem several times before asking the students to suggest a possible title or several titles.
- Accept all responses and compile a blackboard summary. Students must give reasons for their choices and these must be based on the language and imagery of the poem.
- Discuss the students' choices before comparing them with the poet's. Whose is the best and why? Does a poem need a title? Did the title come first, providing a framework for an idea, or did the poet write a poem and then give it a title?

Alfred, Lord Tennyson's 'The Eagle' could be used for this activity. Alternatively, or as a comparison, Ted Hughes's 'Eagle', which presents a different, dramatic and somewhat gory picture of the same bird of prey, could be used.

The Eagle

He clasps the crag with crooked hands;
Close to the sun in lonely lands,
Ringed with the azure world, he stands.

The wrinkled sea beneath him crawls;
He watches from his mountain walls,
And like a thunderbolt he falls.

Alfred, Lord Tennyson[11]

Eagle

Big wings dawns dark.
The Sun is hunting.
Thunder collects, under granite eyebrows.

The horizons are ravenous.
The dark mountain has an electric eye.
The sun lowers its meat-hook.

His spread fingers measure a heaven,
then a heaven.
His ancestors worship only him,
And his children's children cry to him
alone.

His trapeze is a continent.
The Sun is looking for fuel
With the gaze of a guillotine.

And already the White Hare crouches at
the sacrifice,
Already the Fawn stumbles to offer
herself up
And the Wolf-Cub weeps to be chosen.

The huddle-shawled lightning-faced
warrior
Stamps his shaggy-trousered dance
On an altar of blood.

Ted Hughes[12]

Voice from the Vault

This activity draws upon an ABC radio program. Students can read some lines from a favourite poet (this may involve some biographical research) and the class has to guess his/her identity. Some of these may be long dead, such as Tennyson, Alfred Noyes and Edward Lear, or more recent poets, such as Spike Milligan, Shel Silverstein, Jack Davis or Oodgeroo Noonuccal. The choice of poet could celebrate a special event, such as the poet's birthday!

Poem Posters

Have your students make attractive poetry posters in pairs or small groups. These can consist of favourite poems or a collection on a specific theme (the poster could be shaped to represent the theme). Add some artwork to set off the text. Posters can then be displayed in the classroom, corridors, library, outside the Principal's office or staffroom. Such public displays can convert indifferent students (and staff!) to poetry, particularly if the selected poems provoke curiosity and discussion.

Posters for special occasions

Posters containing poems about grandparents can be displayed on 'Grandparents' Day' and a poster display of students' own poetry can be displayed during Education Week. To promote tolerance and understanding, students can create posters containing poems written by Aboriginal writers and students and display them during NAIDOC Week. Poems relating to different cultures can be displayed on Harmony Day as well as on particular festival days/periods, such as Ramadan, Yom Kippur and Chinese New Year.

Wanted! posters

To encourage students to read more widely and, perhaps, to wean them off funny, crude and short poems, 'Wanted' posters can be designed by you or your students with titles such as 'Wanted: a poem about the wind', 'a poem about the sea', 'a poem about drought' and so on. Other headings could include 'Wanted: a poem that made you sad or happy', 'a poem that surprised you' or 'a poem you could not make sense of'. Students will be able to suggest other topics for these posters.

Poetry Friezes

Have the students prepare a frieze to be displayed around the room. Select an episodic poem, such as a ballad or long narrative (eg. Alfred Noyes, 'The Highwayman'). Allocate a section of the poem to each student or small group and have them illustrate it, including the text in their design.

Poetry Week

Dedicate a school week (or month!) to a celebration of poetry. This could coincide with the National Poetry Day in September. Decorate the rooms and corridors with colourful posters, balloons and mobiles with poems written on them and slogans promoting poetry. Have displays of personal and class anthologies and students' writing in the school foyer and library. Invite a local bookseller to bring poetry books for sale! Invite a poet(s) to the school and organise performances by the school poetry troupe (see Chapter 4). However, remember that poetry should be celebrated every day and avoid making such a poetry festival your only coverage of this particular literary genre!

Engaging with Poets

Although students can be exposed to a number of poets during the year, there will always be those who become almost besotted with a particular one. Anthologies used in the classroom and available in the library will usually have only one or two poems by each poet. To satisfy a particular interest, students should be encouraged to seek out other poems by the poet, compile separate anthologies of a number of their works and, perhaps, research some biographical details. They could also write to the poet (providing he/she is still alive) and invite them to visit the school. As Adrian Mitchell says:

If you want to learn
How to talk to grass
Or dance the giraffe
Or imitate glass
Invite a poet
Into your class.

Adrian Mitchell[13]

The young student in Creech's *Love that Dog*[14] who begins by being averse to poetry is slowly turned around by his enthusiastic, supportive teacher. The turning point comes when he is read a poem by Walter Dean Myers and he is instantly 'turned on'. Encouraged by his teacher, he writes to the poet inviting him to the school. His lengthy letter is a delight and well worth reading to a class.

It is important to give students some guidelines before they write their letters to poets. Never ask the poet to interpret or explain their work. They won't because it is up to the reader to seek the meaning. As T.S. Eliot once said in reply to this writer's question – 'If that's what it means to you, then that's what it is!' Have the students tell the poet why they enjoyed a particular poem(s) and how it made them feel.

Before inviting a poet to the school, students need to familiarise themselves with their poetry and prepare interesting and relevant questions. Refer to Libby Gleeson's guidelines[15] on how to invite authors. Hopefully, the visiting poet will not endure the experience in Steven Herrick's 'The Poetry Visitor'.

The Poetry Visitor

Yesterday
a poet came to our school
and read lots of his poems.
Some were funny,
some sad,
some even made Ms Stevrakis laugh,
      especially the one about kissing.
At the end, Ms Stevrakis suggested
we ask the poet questions about his poetry.
After a long silence,
Rachel asked, "how much money do you make?"
Mathew asked, "where do you live?"
Sarah asked, "how old are you?"
Tran asked, "can you speak Vietnamese?"
Sam asked, "how come you've got a bald head?"
And Peter asked, "can I go to the toilet please?"

Steven Herrick[16]

Audio-visual Presentations

Ask your students to prepare slides, overhead transparencies, digital photos or videos and choose appropriate music to accompany their presentation of a poem. The presentation could take the form of a choral reading, mime or dramatisation.

References

1   Fox, G & Merrick, B (1983) 'Thirty-six things to do with a poem' in Mallick, D & Jenkins, G (eds.) *Poetry in the Classroom*. St Clair Press.

2   Herrick, S (1998) *Poetry to the Rescue*. University of Queensland Press. © Steven Herrick. Reprinted with kind permission from the poet.

3   Thurman, J (1977) *Flashlight and other Poems*. Penguin

4   Reeves, J & Ardizzone, E (ill.) (1987) *The Wandering Moon and Other Poems*. Puffin Books.

5   Hayhoe, M (1992) 'Poetry and politics', in Thomson, J (ed.), *Reconstructing Literature Teaching*, AATE, Adelaide.

6   in Williams, WE *Thomas Hardy*

7   Author cannot be traced.

8   Manning, M & O'Neill, J (1994) *New Ways into Poetry*. Oxford University Press p49.

9   Graves, R (1986) *Robert Graves: Collected Poems*. Guild Press

10 Hayhoe, M *op.cit.* p110.

11 in Maynard, J (ed.) and Garns, A (ill.) (2003) *Alfred, Lord Tennyson – Poems for Young People*. Sterling.

12 Hughes, T (2003) *The Hawk in the Rain*. Faber.

13 Mitchell, A & Littlewood, V (ill.) (1993) *The Thirteen Secrets of Poetry*. Simon & Schuster.

14 Creech, S (2001) *Love That Dog*. Bloomsbury.

15 Gleeson, L (1996) *How's your etiquette with authors?* PEN104. PETA.

16 Herrick, S (1997) *My Life, My Love, My Lasagne*. University of Queensland Press. © Steven Herrick. Reprinted with kind permission from the poet.

4

Giving Voice to Poetry

A word is dead
When it is said,
    Some say.

I say it just
Begins to live
    That day.

Emily Dickinson[1]

Most students enjoy listening to poetry being read aloud to them by enthusiastic teachers, visiting poets or competent classmates. Many enjoy silent reading of poetry they find in anthologies and some enjoy writing their own poems. There is, however, no doubt that *all* students enjoy saying poetry out loud – individually, in small groups or as a whole class.

Since reading poetry out loud is the prime element in experiencing poetry, it is vital that teachers lift the words off the page and bring them to life by providing opportunities for students to actively participate in choral reading, multi-voice reading and dramatic performance of poetry. The benefits of this 'say-out loudness' of a poem's words and sounds include:

- allowing *all* students to experience the sheer kinaesthetic or musical pleasure which the articulation of poetic words involves and "letting their tongues going curling around the palpable words plump as plums in the mouth";[2]
- providing collective pleasure in "the delight of utterance";[3]
- creating a feeling of safety in numbers;
- fostering a spirit of cooperation in which the less-proficient students receive support from their peer group;
- catering for individual differences;

- allowing students who may have reading difficulties to experience success;
- developing confidence and competence in speaking to an audience;
- providing an indirect way of 'studying' the structure of a poem;
- drawing students' attention to poetic uses of language;
- deepening their understanding and appreciation of poetic forms;
- assisting students to interpret poetry through the preparation, presentation and evaluation of their own performances; and
- improving physical health. In one of his recent talks on ABC radio, Dr Karl Kruszelnicki went so far as to say that medical research indicates that reading aloud or chanting poetry can actually help your heart.

Poems for Reading Aloud

Some poems, riddles and chants naturally lend themselves to being spoken aloud or performed. Some, in fact, only come alive when they are voiced.

Tongue twisters

There is really no other way to appreciate tongue twisters than to say them out loud. Although some might dismiss them as trivial, Moira Robinson believes that, since they represent a milestone in a student's language development, they should be treated with "proper regard".[4] Indeed, there is no doubt that the patterning of sound/symbol relationships combined with the rhymes and the manipulation of words in tongue twisters contribute to a student's phonological awareness. More importantly, they are fun!

The Yak

Yickity- yackity, yickity-yak
The yak has a scriffly, scraffily back:
Some yaks are brown and some yaks are black,
yickity- yackity, yickity-yak.

Sniggildy-snaggildy, sniggildy-snag.
The yak is all covered with shiggildy-shag;
He walks with a ziggildy-zaggildy-zag
sniggildy-snaggildy, sniggildy-snag.

Yickity- yackity, yickity-yak
The yak has a scriffly, scraffily back:
Some yaks are brown and some yaks are black,
yickity-yackity, yickity-yak.

Jack Prelutsky[5]

Friendly Freddy Fuddlestone

Friendly Fredrick Fuddlestone
Could fiddle on his funny bone.
When Freddy fiddled
Foolishly fast,
He found his father
Frankly aghast.
Friendly Fredrick Fuddlestone
Kept fiddling on his funny bone,
His furious father
Would flatly forbid it,
Which, of course,
Is why young Freddy did it.

Arnold Lobel[6]

Other well known tongue twisters include 'Peter Piper', 'She Sells Seashells by the Seashore', 'Betty Botter' and 'Woodchuck'. Why not have students try a tongue twister in a language other than English, such as the Portugese tongue twister, 'Sparrow'.

Sparrow

Pardal pardo porque pairas?
Eu pairo e pairarei
Porque sou o pardal pardo,
Parlador d'el-rei.

Yellow sparrow, why d'you prattle?
I prattle and prattling will
Because I'm the yellow sparrow,
Royal prattler of King Will.[7]

Chants

In *Squashed Bananas, Mouldy Sultanas*, Jeni Wilson and Lynda Cutting define a chant as "language with energy".[8] The success of chants with students and adults can be attributed to the repetitive, rhyming words and to the clapping, slapping and stamping that usually accompanies them. They also tend to be very loud!

Most students will be familiar with chants as they hear or use them in a range of situations for a variety of purposes. Their earliest experience of chants may well have occurred in a 'learning to read' program where they are often used to develop phonemic awareness. I remember my young six-year-old granddaughter chanting the following rhyme with great gusto while vigorously slapping her thighs. I do not know how much this rhyme contributed to her reading skills but I do know how much she enjoyed it.

Old mother witch
Fell in a ditch
Found a penny
And thought she was rich!

Chants also form an integral part of the culture of the playground where young children use them not only for their games but also just for the joy of making a loud noise! The inventiveness and irreverent humour of their chants and rhymes have been well chronicled by June Factor in *All Right Vegemite!* and *Far Out Brussel Sprout!*. Recently I overheard the following being enthusiastically and energetically chanted by a group of six-year-olds in the school playground.

Ya! Ya! I lost my bra
I lost it in my boyfriend's car!

Inky pinky, pen and inky,
I smell a dirty stinky!

Now, I am not suggesting that we use these examples in the classroom but by providing young students with opportunities to chant rhymes we acknowledge the language and culture of the playground.

People of all ages regularly chant at sporting contests and I am sure that all of us have heard the chant of 'Aussie, Aussie, Aussie, Oi, Oi, Oi' or 'We will, we will rock you'. Similarly, many street protest marches ring with the sound of 'What do we want? When do we want it? NOW!'. Chants also play an important part in religious rituals and meditation practices.

CHANTS TO USE IN THE CLASSROOM

Miss Mary

Miss Mary
Mack
Mack
Mack
all dressed in
black
black
black[9]

Also to be found in Michael Rosen's *A Spider Bought a Bicycle and Other Poems for Young Children* are 'Miss Polly' and 'Jelly on the Plate', both of which are suitable for chanting. Colin Thiele's 'Hamburgers' lends itself to chanting and would appeal if 'performed' just before recess or lunch and 'Thumping, Stumping' could be chanted just before the end of the school day.

Hamburgers

Hamburgers big and Hamburgers small,
Hamburgers pictured and hung on the wall,
Hamburgers jolly and round and fat,
Hamburgers domed like a bowler hat,
Hamburgers served with onion and cheese,
Hamburgers trying their hardest to please,
Hamburgers saucy and Hamburgers plain,
Hamburgers hearty in sunshine or rain,
Hamburgers plump and Hamburgers tall,
The people of Hamburg are Hamburgers all.

Colin Thiele[10]

Thumping, stumping,
Bumping, jumping.

Thumping, stumping, bumping, jumping,
Ripping, nibbing, tripping, skipping,
All the way home.

Popping, clopping, stopping, hopping,
Stalking, chalking, talking, walking,
All the way home.

Anon[11]

Students could also be introduced to chants used by different cultures, such as Bengali and Aboriginal rain chants and the Guyanese 'Skipping Rope Wedding Chant' in the anthology edited by John Agard and Grace Nichols *From Mouth to Mouth: Oral Poems from around the World.*

Raps

If poetry, generally, has lost some of its appeal, the current popularity of rap and hip-hop has done much to revive the fortunes of oral poetry. Variously described as 'graffiti for the ears' and 'speech chanted to funky music', its regular 4 X 4 rhythm, syncopated rhyming, stream-of-consciousness lines, incredible energy, and its often powerful messages have, as one writer said, "done the unthinkable: made poetry cool again".[12] Rappers come from a variety of backgrounds. Just as the African-Americans developed blues music after the American Civil War, rap and hip-hop often reflect the problems facing the working class, the migrant, the poor and the black. Perhaps the Melbourne poet Pi O best summed it up when he said "rap poetry in this country came out of the working class, street-wise, migrant, disempowered and alienated".[13]

Since it is so popular and contemporary, I believe that it is almost imperative to use raps in the classroom. Raps allow all students to improvise words and music that express their hopes, fears, anger and frustration. The positive effect that rap 'poetry' has already had on young Aboriginal students in NSW is reflected in the emergence of groups such as Murdi Rampage and the Boggabilla Thriller. Many of these students have dropped out of school, have been put on partial attendance schemes or have broken the law yet have displayed exceptional talents and abilities in writing and performing rap. Clearly, their success can inspire students for whom school seems an irrelevance. Similarly, raps performed by inner-city Vietnamese students might well resonate with many students from non-English speaking backgrounds.

Since most contemporary rap poetry carries strong political messages, it is not really suitable for younger students. There are, however, many raps which appeal to primary-aged students, including Wes Magee's delightful 'Boneyard Rap'.

Boneyard Rap

This is the rhythm
of the boneyard rap,
knuckle bones click
and hand bones clap,
finger bones flick
and thigh bones slap
when you're doing the rhythm
of the boneyard rap
WOOOOOOOOOO! (slowly raise arms/hands)

Wes Magee[14]

You will find a wide variety of raps in the following books:

- Benjamin Zephaniah *Talking Turkeys* – full of powerful and provocative raps that students will love and are delightful when read aloud
- John Foster (ed.) *Ready, Steady, Rap* – includes a grandma rap, dentist rap, 'brudda' Brad and a beach holiday rap
- Susan Hill (ed.) *Raps and Rhymes*
- Susan Hill (ed.) *Jump For Joy: More Raps and Rhymes*
- Ann Baker and Johnny Baker (eds.) *Raps and Rhymes and Maths*
- Monkey Mark *Raps for Little Fullas*
- Monkey Mark *Raps for Big Fullas*
- Linton Kwesi Johnson, 'Reggae Sounds'.[15]

Finally, it is important to remember that even very young children can write and perform their own rap poetry.

Choral reading

Choral reading, where students speak in unison, should form an integral part of any poetry program. Although chanting and rapping can also be spoken in unison, they tend to depend on informal, improvised words and music whereas what I refer to as 'choral reading' involves speaking the words of a poem – either a well known, published work, or one that the students have written themselves.

Encourage your students to select poems that they wish to read aloud as a whole class. You may have to select poems for the very young students but, once students are competent readers, they are quite capable of choosing poems for choral reading. Although they may need some guidance, highly motivated students will generally select a variety of poems, ranging from the light and humorous to the serious and mysterious – almost invariably, they will have a strong rhythm. Once a poem has been selected for reading aloud, you must ensure that the students practise it. A bad choral reading (a low mutter which nobody can hear) can quickly destroy a poem!

The following points of performance need to be considered.

- Timing is vital. All students must start together (eg. on the count of three).
- Pacing needs to be practised so that the reading does not drag by having students wait for each other to catch up.
- Students need to speak loudly (except where a line demands a softer voice), clearly and confidently.
- Since there is nothing drearier than flat monotone reading, demonstrate how to read a poem with expression, how to use the pause effectively, how to emphasise certain words, phrases and sentences and, where necessary, how to pronounce an accent.
- Encourage students to use appropriate gestures, facial expressions and movement, but allow plenty of room for improvisation.
- Consider using background music to set a mood or create an atmosphere. You might like to use Mick Gowar's *Carnival of the Animals*.[16] This book contains poems written to accompany the musical suite of the same name by the French composer Camille Saint-Saens.
- A kettledrum can be used as a device of punctuation and as a means of achieving suspense, climax and intensification.[17]
- Have students select or compose their own music to accompany the reading.
- Delete words or lines that may mar the performance.
- To increase the motivation, determine who is to be the audience for the choral reading. Another class, children in hospital, men and women in nursing homes or a full school assembly provide students with 'real' audiences.
- Record the early efforts on tape. Students will quickly identify the areas in need of further practice.

- Lastly, if the choral reading of a particular poem is not working and the enthusiasm and enjoyment wane, drop it and choose another one!

Most poems can be translated into choral reading but the ones that work best, particularly with younger students, are action rhymes, involving lots of gestures, facial expressions and body movements. Kindergarten students have, within a week, been able to quite confidently and enthusiastically perform the 'Doctor Knickerbocker' poem (from memory!) for the school assembly. To make the poem more rhythmic and dramatic I leave out 'doctor' at the beginning and end of the poem. You could also consider omitting the 'Wipe wipe' lines as they do not work as well as the other actions.

> Dr Knickerbocker, Knickerbocker number nine,
> Loves to dance to the rhythm of time,
> Now let's get the rhythm of the hands
>> CLAP CLAP
> Now we've got the rhythm of the hands
>> CLAP CLAP
> Now let's get the rhythm of the feet
>> STAMP STAMP
> Now we've got the rhythm of the feet
>> STAMP STAMP
> Now let's get the rhythm of the eyes
>> WIPE WIPE
> Now we've got the rhythm of the eyes
>> WIPE WIPE
> Now let's get the rhythm of the dance
>> WIGGLE WIGGLE
> Now we've got the rhythm of the dance
>> WIGGLE WIGGLE
>> CLAP CLAP,
>> STAMP STAMP,
>> WIPE WIPE,
>> WIGGLE WIGGLE.
> Now we're dancing to the rhythm of time,
> Doctor Knickerbocker,
>> Knickerbocker number nine.

Anon[18]

Another poem that I use with five- and six-year-olds is 'Walking through the Jungle'[19]. This poem has a refrain that they learn relatively easily and the last line 'Looking for his tea' is repeated at the end of each stanza. Often, without prompting, the students improvise the actions, such as 'What can I see?' (hand to eye) and 'What can I hear' (hand to ear) as well as the movements and noises of each animal. I shall never forget the growls of the tigers – vicious and toothless!

To really appreciate and enjoy the 'mouth music' of poetry, select poems that have strong rhythms, infectious rhymes and make good use of alliteration and onomatopoeia. The poem 'Grim and Gloomy' is one of my favourites! It has it all – magnificent use of language, invented words, rhyme (end and internal), repetition, alliteration, assonance and onomatopoeia. I really do not believe that any student should leave school without having read this poem out loud.

Grim and Gloomy

Oh, grim and gloomy,
So grim and gloomy
Are the caves beneath the sea.
Oh, rare but roomy
And bare and boomy,
Those salt sea caverns be.

Oh, slim and slimy
Or grey and grimy
Are the animals of the sea.
Salt and oozy
And safe and snoozy
The caves where those animals be.

Hark to the shuffling,
Huge and snuffling,
Ravenous, cavernous, great sea-beasts!
But fair and fabulous,
Tintinnabulous,
Gay and fabulous are their feasts.

Ah, but the queen of the sea,
The querulous, perilous sea!
How the curls of her tresses
The pearls on her dresses,
Sway and swirl in the waves,
How cosy and dozy
How sweet ring-arosy
Her bower in the deep-sea caves!

Oh, rare but roomy
And bare and boomy
Those caverns under the sea,
And grave and grandiose,
Safe and sandiose
The dens of her denizens be.

James Reeves[20]

Some other suggestions for choral reading include:
- Ogden Nash, 'The Wendigo'[21]
- Lewis Carroll, 'Jaberwocky'[22]
- Steven Herrick, 'Lost in the Mist'[23]
- T.S. Eliot, 'Macavity: The Mystery Cat'[24]
- Irene McLeod, 'Lone Dog'[25]
- Spike Milligan, 'On the Ning, Nang, Nong'[26]
- Robert Louis Stevenson, 'Windy Nights'[27]
- Hillaire Belloc, 'Tarantella'.[28]

Multi-voice reading

Instead of the whole class reading with one voice, poems can be read using the voices of individual speakers alone or in combination. Monologue poems such as Dulcie Meddows' 'Hello Grandma'[29] can be adapted for several voices. Also, dialogue/conversation poems such as Elizabeth Honey's 'Clothesblind'[30] and 'What will I wear?',[31] and Margaret Porter's 'Are you receiving me?'[32] work well with young students. Multi-voice reading involves considerable organisation, but since the students are involved in all aspects of performance, it is well worth the effort.

The following points should be considered when preparing a multi-voice reading.

- Before students select a poem for multi-voice reading, provide them with some guidelines, such as how many voices are required and the ways in which the poem might be interpreted and presented.
- Some poems will involve the whole class reading different lines but others will be performed by small groups.
- Have the students allocate parts. Where the poem needs a 'leader', you may need to suggest a student who is a competent and confident speaker.
- Provide each student with a copy of the poem to be read aloud and have the students annotate it with comments that relate to rhythmic variation, change of pace, modification of pause, volume and tone. These comments will reflect their interpretation of the poem.
- Ask students to consider whether music, movement, gestures or slides will 'improve' their reading and, if so, what they should use.

You will need to provide students with a range of poetry that relies on a number of different voices for its effectiveness. Look for poems that meet the following criteria for multi-voice readings.

- Poems that have repetitive refrains, where one or two confident students read the stanzas while the rest of the class chants the refrain or chorus. The 'Witches' Spell' from Macbeth is one example.
- Poems that have distinct sections, where groups can each be assigned one section of the poem to read, such as Kit Wright's 'My Dad, Your Dad'[33] and 'Stop That Noise'.[34]
- Poems that can be read by one person, with the rest of the class repeating or 'echoing' line by line, such as 'Army Song'.

Army Song

I don't know but I've been told (echo)
Sally's legs are made of gold (echo)
Sound off (echo)
1 2 3 4 (echo)

- Poems that call for a response, such as Christina Rossetti's 'What is Pink?', 'Soldier, Soldier Won't you Marry me?',[35] or 'Two Pilots'.[36] The nursery rhyme 'Who killed Cock Robin?' also lends itself well to multi-voice reading.
- Poems that build in intensity as voices are added with each succeeding line, such as 'There Was an Old Lady Who Swallowed a Fly'. The whole class reads the opening lines and the final line of each stanza as well as the last two lines of the poem.

The following poems, 'Mum' and 'Dad', lend themselves well to multi-voice reading and would be ideal to perform at a school assembly, attended by parents. There are enough lines for every child to read one each and the whole class can join in with the last line of every stanza as well as the last three lines of each poem. Stand children in the order of the line to be read so that they do not lose their place. Ensure that they pause between the lines and the 'punch line' and draw out the 'well'. It is also important that they do not continue to speak over the laughter from the audience!

Mum

She's a:

Sadness stealer.
  Cut-knee healer.
    Hug-me-tighter.
      Wrongness righter.
      Gold-star carer.
      Chocolate sharer
        (well sometimes!)

  Hamster feeder.
  Bedtime reader.
Great game player.
Night-fear slayer.
Treat dispenser.
Naughty sensor
  (how come she always knows?)

    She's my
  Never-glum,
    Constant-chum,
      Second-to-none,
        (We're under her thumb!)
          Mum!

Polly Peters[37]

Dad

He's a:

    Tall-story weaver.
      Full-of-fib Fever.
      Bad-joke teller.
        Ten decibel yeller.
        Baggy-clothes wearer.
      Pocket-money bearer.
     Nightmare banisher.
    Hurt-heart vanisher …

  Bear hugger.
 Biscuit mugger.
Worry squasher.
Noisy nosher.
Lawn mower.
Smile sower …

Football mad.
  Fashion sad.
    Not half bad.
      So glad I had
          My
            Dad!

Andrew Fusek Peters and Polly Peters[38]

Dramatisation

Dramatising poetry is a very worthwhile activity, especially for older students. Given the impetus of a disciplined activity with a defined end in view, students generally find the experience an enjoyable, useful and somewhat demanding way to explore the meaning of a particular poem.

Narrative poems, which are often quite long, can be successfully dramatised. Unlike other forms of reading aloud where the students generally improvise sound effects and simple props, dramatisation involves lengthy planning and numerous rehearsals. Having selected a suitable poem, the students have to consider all aspects of the production. To begin this process and to demonstrate the roles they need to consider, I usually roll through the credits of a film. The excitement mounts quickly as they brainstorm various aspects of their proposed production, such as costumes, make-up, lighting, sound effects, props and scenery. Older students invariably suggest that we conduct auditions, 'hire' a director, stage manager and lighting crew and someone to provide the catering!

Although some critics believe that poems such as 'The Man from Ironbark' are too difficult (especially for students who may not have the cultural background) because of the language and the humour, I have not found this to be the case. I tell them the story first and explain the practical joke. We also look at peculiar occupations, such as 'peeler men', discuss descriptive terms, such as 'gilded youths', and the way that barbers do (or did) shave a customer. Then we read the poem together, allocate parts and plan how and when we will perform it. Because this poem is full of action (including a fight scene) and humour, it is usually performed with much verve and vigour. Although there are few female roles (except as part of the city crowd), I have found that girls readily accept male roles (these days, many shearers are women!). One Sydney school successfully got around this 'problem' by using masks for the characters. The role of the narrator can be read by the whole class.

Some other 'poems' that lend themselves to dramatisation include:

- Gillian Rubinstein, 'Sharon, keep your hair on'[39]
- Gillian Rubinstein, 'Hooray for the Kafe Karaoke!'[40]
- Edward Lear 'The Owl and the Pussy Cat'[41]
- Karla Kuskin, 'James and the Rain' (for younger students)[42]
- Alfred Noyes, 'The Highwayman'[43]
- Graeme Base My Grandma Lived in Gooligulch: A Small Play for Furry Animals – this popular children's book is now available as a playscript and includes sound and stage tips.[44]

Reader's Theatre

If you do not have the time or the inclination to mount a dramatic presentation of a poem, you can always use a reader's theatre "as a bridge between choral reading and a fully staged performance".[45] Rather than learn their parts, students read from scripts, speak directly to their audience and generally use only a few actions, gestures and props. Also, they do not have to dress up. They do, however, need to allocate roles and decide on how they will interpret and present their poem.

Poetry Troupe

I was first introduced to this idea by an enthusiastic teacher-librarian, who made poetry reading and sharing a regular part of her library lessons. She quickly acquired a group of young poetry devotees who read lots of poems, borrowed poetry books and delighted in reading poetry out loud. Invited to talk to a university class, the teacher impulsively took her little band of poetry lovers with her. They read poems to the students. It was a great success and so the idea of a poetry troupe was born!

Some years ago, I was fortunate enough to see a poetry troupe in action at a poetry festival in Sydney. Vivienne Nicoll-Hatton brought a troupe of young students to perform for the poets, teachers and parents who were gathered together on the day. Max Fatchen was so impressed that he responded with a poem that he wrote on the spot.

> We older poets can be so tiring
> But hearing you is so
> > inspiring
>
> This is, I think, a stirring
> > fact
> How well young people read
> > and act
>
> We poets have but words
> > to give
> But you the children
> > make them live.

Max Fatchen[46]

So, for those students who just cannot get enough of reading poetry and speaking it out loud, try organising a poetry troupe. They could be your school's travelling troubadours and perform for a range of audiences throughout your local area.

Poetry Concert

Whereas most of the reading aloud will occur within the classroom, it is important to provide students with other audiences. Where choral reading, multi-voice reading and dramatisation are taking place across the school, a poetry concert could be staged for a wider audience. What better way to celebrate the last day of term or spend an enchanted evening with families and community members in attendance? Tickets could be sold and the proceeds spent on poetry books for the school library!

To be successful, it is important that the concert program is fast-moving, includes a range of poems (light and humorous, serious and sad, dramatic and reflective) is varied in presentation (choral reading, multi-voice, rapping) and includes some music, dance and perhaps slides or backdrops produced by the students. Remember to include some poems written by the students temselves.

References

1   Prelutsky, J (ed.) (1985) *The Walker Book of Poetry for Children*. Walker Books, London.

2   Wilner, I (1979) 'Making poetry happen: birth of a poetry troupe' in *Children's Literature in Education* vol.10:2, p87.

3   Britton, J (1983) 'Reading and writing poetry' in Arnold, R (ed.) *Timely Voices: English Teaching in the Eighties*. Oxford University Press, Melbourne p5.

4   Robinson, M (1984) *Children's Playground Rhymes, Chants and Traditional Verse*. Primary English Notes, PETA, Sydney p8.

5   Prelutsky, J (ed.) (1985) *op.cit.*

6   Lobel, A (1985) *Whiskers and Rhymes*. Greenwillow Books.

7   Agard, J, Nichols, G (eds.) (2004) *From Mouth to Mouth: Oral Poems from Around the World*. Walker Books p87.

8   Cutting, L & Wilson, J (1992) *Squashed Bananas, Mouldy Sultanas – a diet of chants*. Oxford University Press.

9   Rosen, M (ed.) (1987) *A Spider Bought a Bicycle and other poems for young children*. Kingfisher.

10 Thiele, C (1989) *Poems in my luggage*. Puffin Australia. Reprinted with kind permission from the poet.

11 Rumble, A (ed.) (1989) *Is A Caterpillar Ticklish?* Puffin Books.

12 *Sydney Morning Herald* 3/1/04

13 *ibid.*

14 Moses, B (ed.) (2003) *Poems Out Loud*. Hodder Children's Books. Reprinted with permission.

15 Mitchell, A (ed.) (1996) *The Orchard Book of Poems*. Orchard Books.

16 Gowar, M & Buchanan, G (ill.) (1994) *Carnival of the Animals*. Puffin Books.

17 Summerfield, G (1983) 'Poetry and performance: a lesson', in Mallick, D & Jenkins, G (eds.) *Poetry in the Classroom*. St Clair Press, Sydney p92.

18 Rosen, M (ed.) *op.cit.*

19 Kuffner, P (1999) *The Toddler's Busy Book*. Meadowbrook Press.

20 Reeves, J (1987) *The Wandering Moon and Other Poems*. Puffin Books. Reprinted courtesy Laura Cecil Literary Agency.

21 Blake, Q (1996) *The Penguin Book of Nonsense Verse*. Puffin Poetry.

22 *ibid.*

23 Herrick, S (1998) *Poetry to the Rescue*. University of Queensland Press.

24 Eliot, TS (2001) *Old Possum's Book of Practical Cats*. Faber.

25 Prelutsky, J (ed.) (1985) *op.cit.*

26 Blake, Q (1996) *op.cit.*

27 Rosen, M (ed.) (1991) *The Kingfisher Book of Children's Poetry*. Kingfisher.

28 *ibid.*

29 Scott-Mitchell, C, Griffith, K (eds.) & Rogers, G (ill.) (2002) *100 Australian poems for children*. Random House, Australia.

30 Honey, E (1993) *Honey Sandwich*. Allen & Unwin.

31 Honey, E (1998) *Mongrel Doggerel*. Allen & Unwin.

32 Harvey, A (ed.) (1995) *He Said, She Said, They Said. Poetry in Conversation*. Puffin.

33 *ibid*.

34 Cutting, L & Wilson, J (1992) *op.cit*.

35 Ireson, B (ed.) (1970) *The Young Puffin Book of Verse*. Puffin Books.

36 Rosen, M (ed.) (1987) *op.cit*.

37 Peters, A F and Peters, P (2001) *Sadderday and Funday*. Hodder Children's Books. Reprinted with kind permission from the poet.

38 *ibid*. Reprinted with kind permission from the poets.

39 Rubinstein, G (1996) *Sharon, keep your hair on*. Random House Australia.

40 Rubinstein, G (1998) *Hooray for the Kafe Karaoke!* Random House Australia.

41 many editions, including Lear, E & Beck, I (ill.) (1995) *The Owl and the Pussy-Cat*. Corgi.

42 Kuskin, K (1995) *James and the Rain*. Simon and Schuster.

43 in many anthologies, or Noyes. A & Keeping, C (ill.) (1981) *The Highwayman*. Oxford University Press.

44 Base, G (2002). Claremont (Penguin Aust.).

45 Ewing, R, Simons, J & Hertzberg, M (2004) *Beyond the Script: Drama in the Classroom*. PETA, Sydney p83.

46 unpublished, Dec 1 1996 at the PETA Poetry Festival. © Max Fatchen. Reprinted with kind permission from the poet.

5

Writing Poetry: Getting Started

Most poets agree that every child should have the chance to write some poetry at school, not only because they can 'escape' from the more formal language and rigid conventions of factual text types, but also because it allows them to write freely about their personal thoughts, feelings and experiences. Because of poetry's brevity and patterning, it is an attractive mode of writing for most students. In a guided classroom activity, students for whom English is a second language and students who are reluctant writers can write poetry with relative ease and, more importantly, experience success.

The Role of the Teacher in the Writing Process

If we subscribe to the belief that everybody has some poetry in them, it is our duty, as teachers, to provide boundless opportunities for students to let, as Shakespeare said in *Midsummer Night's Dream* 'their imagination body forth', and to let them daringly experiment with language and form. The teacher (and his/her enthusiasm and positive attitude) is, as always, the vital catalyst in this process.

Pre-writing activities

- Provide a range of resources – music, artworks, anthologies and media texts – in order to "jar loose the words inside their heads and set free a flow of ideas".[1]
- Engage in word games. Build word banks of gentle words, strong words, sound words, movement words, and words that carry connotations of approval or disapproval. Display these on the classroom walls together with Jack Ousbey's poem 'Taking Hold'.

Taking Hold

Make words work: make them tell the tale you want to tell.
Let them show who you are and how you feel: use words well.
Move words around: make them step out, march, advance.
Feel the pulse of them, the sway, the spring: make words dance.
Make words sound: hear them loud and clear, listen to their ring.
Hear them hum to each other, catch their tunes: make words sing.
Dig with words: turn up meanings, rake over, hoe.
Uncover buried stories, incantations: make words grow.
Polish words now: make them glint and glimmer, cast a spell.
Ready? Take hold then and dazzle us: wear words well.

Jack Ousbey[2]

- Jointly construct some poems – particularly formulaic ones.
- Encourage, excite and enthuse students – demonstrate confidence in them and their ability to write.
- Have students keep a 'poet's notebook' in which they record words and phrases that interest and intrigue them. Tell them that most writers keep such personal notebooks in which they record their observations, comments and reflections.
- Design some writing guidelines, such as appropriate use of language, and the need to resist the temptation to make personal attacks on family and friends. Remind students to consider their audience when writing.

During writing activities

- The best model for young writers is a teacher who writes poems and shares them with his/her students.
- Avoid 'getting in the way' while students are writing.
- Explain that very few writers 'get it right' in their first draft. Show them some poets' drafts, such as those of Geoff Goodfellow[3] and Ted Hughes,[4] and remind them that most writers write many drafts.
- Respond sensitively, personally and positively to students' ideas and efforts.
- Never give marks to this form of writing! Once, during an inspection of a

teacher in an inner-city school, I came across the following poem (I have edited it here) written by a nine-year-old boy in response to the theme of 'loneliness'.

Sometimes I feel lonely when Mum's late home from work
And when someone like Gran dies
And when I haven't got a friend

The teacher had written (in the most beautiful script) 'More care needed with spelling and expression' 4/10! I wonder if that young boy ever wrote anything 'meaningful' again.

- To demonstrate that you have really engaged with the writer you could adopt some of Ms Kranke's superb, thoughtful comments in *Troy Thompson's Excellent Peotry Book*. She responds to Troy's poems with comments such as "I was very moved and had a little cry" and "You have made the mythical beast [a sabre toothed tiger] 'come alive' through your words. I found myself gripped in panic and excitement by the cave people's plight. Who needs Steven Spielberg?" She also tries to wean him off using "bottoms, poo and rude smells" by giving him 10/10 when he eschews such words.[5]

- Allow students plenty of time to think, reflect, discuss, write numerous drafts, edit, revise and polish their poems. As the Caribbean poet John Agard points out, "Even if a poem comes fairly quickly, there's always chipping and pruning to be done" and, in his case, the process takes months.[6]

- Edit with care and consideration and be mindful of the Russian poet, Kornei Chukovsky's observation that the 'corrections' made by teachers to students' verses are often worse than the original version!

- Heed Eric Finney's advice summed up in his 'Poem about Writing a Poem'.

Poem about Writing a Poem

'Write a poem,' she says
'About anything you like.'
You can practically feel the class all
*   thinking,*
'On your blooming bike!'
A poem! I'll tell you one thing:
Mine's not going to rhyme.
A poem between now and playtime!
There's not the time.
In half an hour she'll say,
'Have you done? Hand papers in
And go out.'
I mean does she have the slightest idea
What writing a poem's about?
I mean it's agony:
It's scribbling thoughts

And looking for rhymes
And ways to begin and end:
And giving up in total despair –
'I'm chucking it in the bin.'
But tomorrow it pulls you back again,
And hey, a bit of it clicks!
And you sweat with the words
But it's hopeless again
And it sticks.
And you put it away forever …

But it nags away at the back of your head
And the bits of it buzz and roam,
And maybe – about a century later –
You've got a kind of a poem.

Eric Finney [7]

After writing activities

- Proudly publish the poems – but only if the student gives permission.
- Establish a relationship of trust with students by making sure that their poems are not exposed to an unsympathetic audience.
- Display students' poems in public places.
- Compile an anthology of students' poems.
- Read their poems at the school assembly.
- Enter some of the poems in competitions, such as the Dorothea Mackellar Poetry Awards or the Taronga Foundation Poetry Prize.

Where to Begin?

Although there are always some students who can write poems without a specific stimulus, model or literary framework, most will need some guidance and motivation.

Group poems

A good way to build confidence and have students experience immediate success is to begin with a group poem. As Michael Rosen says, group poems have the advantage of being collective and individual; oral and non-threatening.[8]

I have enjoyed considerable success with Rosen's poem 'Mum Says'. In a Year 7 class in the Snowy Mountains, I gave the first line and almost everyone in the class, enthusiastically, contributed their own. The responses were written quickly on the blackboard by a teacher scribe. I found that by clapping and repeating 'Mum says' at the end of several lines we established a definite rhythm, created a refrain and increased the enjoyment. You could also reverse the order to 'Says Mum!'. Since all the responses seemed rather negative (do your homework, clean your room, walk the dog, don't eat with your mouth open), I added 'Mum says I love you!'. Contributions such as 'Don't piddle on the toilet seat' and 'Don't leave home without your condoms' were amended!

When we were 'happy' with our efforts we read the poem out loud (with sound effects!) and the students were invited to copy it into their books, change it, rearrange it, add to it or write another one on a similar topic, such as 'Dad says', 'Gran says' or 'Hung or Tyr or Pete says'.

FURTHER IDEAS FOR GROUP POEMS

- I used to … but now … (eg. I used to bite my nails but now I don't).
- Out in the playground … (eg. we play handball out in the playground).

- I'm sorry that … (eg. I forgot your birthday, broke the window, called you names, hurt you).
- One day I will … but not today! (eg. One day I will run away but not today).
- Without you … (Look at the last two lines from Adrian Henri's beautiful, moving poem 'Without You' for inspiration here: *Every morning would be like going back to school after a holiday, there'd be no colour in Magic colouring books.*).[9]
- If I were a boy/girl, I would …
  The following group poem was written by an ESL class.

  If I were a boy, I would
    scratch in class
  fight my friends
  wear old clothes
  I'm glad I'm a girl.[10]

- I wish I was … Harris and McFarlane cite Kenneth Koch's idea of starting each line with 'I wish …', followed by three consistent ideas like a cartoon character, a colour and a place.

  I wish I was Wonder Woman in a blue cape dancing with Superman at Jules Bar.[11]

List poems

These poems take the form of a list describing something in detail and are relatively easy to write. They can use the same word to start each line, can be rhymed or written in free verse. Steven Herrick's 'The Ten Commandments (or Ten Things Your Parents Will Never Say!)' is an excellent starting point for a list poem.

The Ten Commandments (or Ten Things Your Parents Will Never Say!)

Let's forget dinner tonight, we'll eat ice-cream instead.
Goodnight children, I'm off to bed. Stay up as late as you want.
No homework tonight, I'm putting all homework in the fireplace immediately.
Children, don't be so quiet. Start yelling, turn the TV up, Start arguing. NOW!
Yes, of course you can have 21 of your friends come over to stay on Saturday night.
  We've got heaps of room.
No, don't listen to the dentist. Lollies and biscuits are good for your teeth.
Yes, that SuperdoopaComputerGame is too expensive
  But let's buy it anyway and we'll put it in your room.
What's that? You broke the kitchen window. Good boy.
Can someone go to the shop for a paper? Here's $100, keep the change.
Yes, I know it's Monday, but why don't we stay home from school anyway?

Steven Herrick[12]

This poem is always an instant success in classrooms as is 'Part Two – The Ten Things Your Teacher Will Never Say'.[13] Most students will eagerly either write another list of ten things their parents or teachers will never say or replace them with ten things their sister/ brother/ grandparent/ friend/ school bully will never say. The teacher might write her/his own poem on the ten things their spouse/ partner/ children/ students will never say.

SOME OTHER TOPICS FOR LIST POEMS

- Irritating sayings, such as the following.
  Isn't it time you thought about bed?
  It must be somewhere.
  Who do you think I am?
  You'd better ask your father.
  Did anybody ask your opinion?
  What did I just say?
  Because I say so!
  Do you think I'm made of money?

- Things I have been doing lately.
  Pretending to go mad
  Eating my own cheeks from the inside[14]

- What ifs ...
  Last night, while I lay thinking here,
  Some whatifs crawled inside my ear ...
  Whatif I start to cry?
  Whatif I get sick and die?[15]

- Things that I love ... the smell of, the look of, the sound of, the feel of and the taste of ...
  The following poems could be read to get students started.
  I like noise.
  The whoop of a boy, the thud of a hoof,
  The hubbub of traffic, the roar of a train,
  The throb of machinery numbing the brain ...[16]

  The joy of smells, too, will never pass;
  I love the scent of new-mown grass,
  The salty tang of a sandy beach,
  And the gentle fragrance of a peach.[17]

- Things that make me furious.
  Students can have great fun writing a list poem about things that they hate and the teacher can join in with his/her own lists (eg. children with mobile

phones, the sound of an i-Pod on somebody else's head, body piercing, heavy metal music blaring from car stereos). However, the poem by the Chilean poet, Teresa de Jesus, should raise the level of discussion beyond 'my brother changing the TV channel' to issues such as children in detention centres, homeless people, senseless acts of violence, racism, bullying.

When I come upon a child
sad, dirty, skinny
it makes me furious!

When I see food
tossed into the garbage
and a poor man poking around in case
it isn't rotten yet
it makes me furious!

When a toothless woman
hunched and old tells me
she's 26
it makes me furious!

When the poor wait
for the rich man to finish his business
to ask him
for last week's salary
it makes me furious!

Teresa de Jesus[18]

Students could also be encouraged to write a follow-up poem on 'What I'm going to do about it'.

- Excuses for not doing one's homework.

I couldn't do my homework.
I had asthma and was wheezing.
I had nosebleeds, measles and heat rash,
with some very painful sneezing,
and itchy skin with blisters –
oh so blotchy red and hivy –
malaria and toothaches,
and a patch of poison ivy,
eight spider bites and hair loss,

and a broken leg with scabies
Rocky Mountain spotted fever,
and a full-blown case of rabies.
I suffered – it was awful –
but I'm feeling better now.
Could I have done my homework?
No, I really don't see how.

Joyce Armor[19]

- Excuses for being late or absent from school.
  Look at Steven Herrick's 'Dear Ms Ginola'[20] and Robert Hull's 'Dear Mrs James' (written in the persona of a child writing a letter to explain her mother's absence from school) as examples of excuse poems.

When writing list poems, students may like to write them as parodies of well known poems, songs, carols and hymns (see Chapter 2).

Sensory poems

A good way to begin poetry writing is to use a sensory poem. Students select an object and describe it in terms of smell, touch, sound, taste (if appropriate) and sight. Adrian Mitchell provides some good advice to young writers, when he says: "If you decide to write about a tree, look at that tree, touch it, smell it, climb it if you can. Write about what makes that tree different from all the other trees in the world".[21] Refer to Chapter 6 for more ideas for writing sensory poems.

Found poems

These are formed from pieces of prose writing 'found' in the environment. Ask students to 'find' newspaper headlines, advertisements, graffiti, slogans and signs and arrange them into a poem. Traffic signs (written and visual) and roadside banners would make a good starting point for a serious or humorous poem. Just imagine what fun your class can have with signs such as 'Stop, Revive, Survive', pictures of koalas, kangaroos, livestock, speed humps and children and 'No overtaking in the tunnel'. Such a writing activity can also help them understand ambiguity!

Metaphor poems

A metaphor involves the figuring or envisaging of one object in terms of another and, by so doing, enables the reader to appreciate the original more clearly and with deeper understanding. It also, according to Colin Thiele "illuminates truths, often with laser-like brightness".[22]

Michael Rosen suggests that if young writers are to write metaphor poems, they should start by collecting those used by children, their families or people on television.[23] Some examples, which could be made into a list poem, might include:

- 'you're a pain in the neck'
- 'my brother is a monster'
- 'our car is an old bomb'
- 'Fred is a goose'.

I believe, however, that students need to be challenged and taken beyond their own environment and oral language to explore new worlds. Seeing balloons as 'wild space animals', the sea as 'a wild dog' or a 'battering ram' forces students to use their imaginations and think about the power of figurative language. Comparing similes and metaphors helps them appreciate the force of a metaphor. Any collection of poetry written by children provides proof that children can write in sustained metaphor (with or without personification).

Lucky dip

Since poetry is about words and imagination, students needed to be provided with many opportunities to play with language. The following is one suggestion worth pursuing.

Prepare cards with a word or phrase on each. You can also buy magnetic poetry kits which contain hundreds of words. You might like to have separate boxes of nouns, verbs, adjectives, adverbs and other parts of speech or just mix them up. In groups of four, students select four or more words and phrases and write a poem which can be sheer nonsense or deeply profound. Before writing, students could discuss a possible topic for their poem or it can just emerge from the words.

Word association game

Many years ago, Roslyn Arnold suggested the following 'activity' as a way into poetry writing. Suggest to your students an evocative word, such as 'misery', 'happiness', 'school', 'birthday' or 'conflict'. Ask students to write down a place, person, colour or idea that the word conjures up in their minds and invite them to write a poem.

Poems for special occasions

Students can collect a range of greeting cards for a variety of occasions, such as birthdays, Mother's Day and Father's Day, Valentine's Day, New Year's Day (Christian, Jewish, Chinese), Halloween, Ramadan, Hannukah. Ask students to critically examine the language used, for example trite rhymes, and the illustrations (sickly sentimental?) and then design their own. I would strongly recommend Doug MacLeod's *On the Cards* for this writing activity.

Poetry and art

Paintings, particularly those by Van Gogh and Bruegel, have inspired many poets to respond with a picture in words and to capture the mood and feelings of a particular artwork. Brian Dunlop's painting, *The Blue Dress*, inspired Libby Hathorn to write poems based on the image of the young girl and these, in turn, led to Stephen Lalor composing music to accompany them.[24]

Students need to be exposed to a wide range of artistic styles and themes in order to write poems in response to an artwork. You could show younger students picture books, many of which have been illustrated by skilled artists. Older students could closely examine the artwork of Shaun Tan, Jeannie Baker, Steven Woolnam, Ron Brooks and Tohby Riddle and select one illustration which interests or intrigues them. As they look at the drawing, collage or painting, they should jot down their feelings and reactions. This can be the basis for writing a poem.

In some instances, they can act as detectives and solve puzzles (such as the patterns and puzzles in Steven Woolman's illustrations for Gary Crew's *The Watertower*) or to find the particular artwork that influenced the illustrator (Jeffrey Smart's artwork *Cahill Expressway* influenced Shaun Tan's *The Lost Thing*). Tohby Riddle's *The Great Escape from the City Zoo* is an excellent stimulus not only for tracing the sources of the illustrations but also for writing poems. At one point in the story, the animal escapees eat at 'Phillies' – an all night diner. Show the students Edward Hopper's painting *Nighthawks* and they will immediately see that Riddle has used it as a model. Then read Julie O'Callaghan's poem 'Nighthawks'. The painting and the poem can be found in Michael and Peter Benton's *Double Vision: Reading Paintings … Reading Poems … Reading Paintings*, a book which is full of imaginative ideas and practical teaching strategies to combine poetry and art.

Nighthawks

The heat and the dark
drive us from apartments
down empty streets
to the all-night diner
where fluorescent lights
illuminate us like tropical fish
in a fish tank.
We sit side by side
listening to glasses clank,
the waiter whistling,
and stare at the concrete outside.
Not looking at our watches
Or counting the cigarettes
And cups of coffee.

Julie O'Callaghan[25]

TEACHING IDEAS

- Since Jeannie Baker's *Window* is a wordless text, students could take any page and write a poem to accompany the picture.
- Buy a series of art postcards from the Art Gallery. In pairs, ask students to discuss the story in the picture and to write a poetic response. Frederick McCubbin's *The Lost Child* or Tom Roberts's *Breakaway* should provoke a wide variety of emotions.

- One poet who was inspired by the paintings of Pieter Bruegel was William Carlos Williams. His poems written in response to *Landscape with the Fall of Icarus* and *Hunters in the Snow* are well worth reading while looking at a print of the original painting. Students can then write their own poems on this or another myth or legend. Also look at W.H. Auden's 'Musée des Beaux Arts' in relation to Bruegel's painting *Landscape with the Fall of Icarus*.[26]
- Aboriginal art often tells a story, and the works are rich in symbolism and imagery. Before having students write poetry in response to this form of art, read them a selection from *Crow Feathers: An Indigenous Collection of Poems and Images*.[27]
- Another useful resource is Quentin Blake's *Tell Me a Picture*, which attempts to bring children and paintings together. Many students will be familiar with his humorous, unforgettable illustrations of the poems of Roald Dahl and Michael Rosen. To understand the relationship between poetry and art, they should look at *The Penguin Book of Nonsense Verse* in which the poems were both selected and illustrated by Quentin Blake.

Writing poems as responses to school activities

Instead of writing a 'review' of a novel read in class or a factual recount of an excursion, ask students to respond in poetry. For example, a Year 1 class in a Blue Mountains school produced this jointly constructed class poem as a response to the film *Alaska*.

Rough fierce wolves howling loud
Playful black bears
Splashing in the river.
Whales cooperating to get food
Crystal ice crashing.
A red fox digging in the sand
Brave eagles flying
Hunters killing with their spears
Fish jumping high
Laying eggs and then dying
We came face to face with the
Wilderness.

Year 1, Blue Mountains Grammar School

A nine-year-old boy wrote a poem in response to reading Emily Rodda's *Rowan of Rin*. Here is his first draft.

Sheba, Sheba you were wrong
John and I did carry on.
When sleep was death and hope was gone
We faced forest and swamp and passed through.
I freed the dragon from its pain
And returned home from the flame.
My love for Star helped me carry on
I was even called 'brave' by John.

Toby Settree (age 9) Warrimoo Public School

Writing Frameworks

To trigger their ideas, experiences and emotions and to develop their confidence and competence, some students may need to be provided with a writing framework. These scaffolds allow students of varying ability, linguistic proficiency and attitude to focus on their ideas and feelings rather than on the mechanics of the poem. It is important, however, to be flexible and not to force students to adhere rigidly to a particular framework.

One way to enable students to reflect on their own experiences, fears, hopes and dreams is to use the following 'I am' framework.

I am

1st stanza

I am ...	*(two special characteristics you have)*
I wonder ...	*(something you are curious about)*
I hear ...	*(a sound you can imagine hearing)*
I want ...	*(an actual desire you have)*
I am ...	*(repeat the first line)*

2nd stanza

I pretend ...	*(something you pretend to do or believe)*
I feel ...	*(a feeling you have about something real or imaginary)*
I touch ...	*(something you can imagine touching)*
I worry ...	*(something you worry about)*
I cry ...	*(something that makes you sad)*
I am ...	*(repeat the first line)*

3rd stanza

I understand ...	*(something you know is true)*
I say ...	*(something you believe in)*
I dream ...	*(something you dream about)*
I try ...	*(something you make an effort to do)*
I hope ...	*(something you hope for)*
I am ...	*(repeat the first line)*

This framework works well with different age groups but you may need to engage in some preliminary discussions before using it.

- Discuss personal traits before writing and brainstorm ideas on the whiteboard. The first reaction of students is to describe their physical characteristics so start to draw students towards describing their inner characteristics and emotions. For example, one student changed her description from 'I am tall and thin' to 'I am seriously sensitive'.
- Because it often tends to spoil the emerging introspection, you might consider dropping the repetition of 'I am' from the end of each stanza.
- Since the poems are so personal, some students may not wish to write about themselves. Give them the opportunity to write in the third person or about a third person or to use a pseudonym. If read aloud by the teacher, the student must give permission and may wish to remain anonymous.
- Do not have students read their own poems aloud. They rarely project the feelings that a good teacher reading can evoke.

I have used the activity described above with students of varying backgrounds across NSW and have been concerned that many students see themselves as failures. Although some focus on physical attributes, others are concerned with wider issues, such as death, the future and social isolation. The following extracts are from 'I am' poems written by Years 8 and 9 students at Collarenebri in north-western NSW, a town with a large Aboriginal community.

I wonder when I die whether I will just vanish or go on to another life
I wonder whether I'll end up in gaol
I wonder why the world is the way it is

I touch lines on a barked tree
And worry that it might feel the same pain as me.

I try to hold my courage
"I try to say goodbye but I choke"

I cry for all living things
I cry when someone dies

I worry about dying
I worry about my brother in gaol
I worry about life

The following poems were written by Year 6 students at a large inner-city school. The students are, generally, drawn from educated, middle-class families.

I am different
I hear laughter
I want to change
But I am different.

I pretend to be someone else
I often feel embarrassed
I touch my breath
I worry about the next day
I cry for others less fortunate than myself
I am different.

I understand that I'm going to die
I say 'Why?'
I dream about my being different
I try to be someone that I am not
I hope that I will change one day
But I am different.

Julian Pattie[28]

I pretend that I live like royalty
I feel death awaiting me
I touch my face
I worry about life and what it will do
I cry when I am sad
I am lost in my own mind.

Finn Stanaway-Dowse[29]

These poems were written by boys – putting paid to the view that 'Boys don't write poetry. Girls do'.[30] They also demonstrate that children's voices can be as powerful as adults'!

Self portraits

Another way of having students write about their personal experiences, fears and feelings is to present them with a framework. This example is based on Steven Herrick's series of poems on 'Joe and Debbie' in *Water Bombs*.[31] Students put themselves in the position of either character and describe themselves aged 9, 14, 16 and 30 years. They can follow the framework of these poems or vary it to suit themselves. Also, they might like to question why the poet writes about Joe at 30 but not Debbie and they might like to speculate as to where they would both be at, say, 42. Start with a framework such as:

My name is Joseph
Or Joe
I'm in Year 5
Mr Dunstan's my teacher
The things I like about school are…
The things I don't like are…
I wish…

Portraits and personalities

Although poems about themselves may provide an easy entry into writing, students can create another character and describe his/her actions, feelings and attitudes while using the personal 'I'. C.J. Dennis's 'The Postman' is a good model to work with.

The Postman

I'd like to be a postman, and walk along the street,
Calling out, 'Good Morning Sir,' to gentlemen I meet;
Ringing every door-bell all along my beat,
In my cap and uniform so very nice and neat,
Perhaps I'd have an umbrella in case of rain or heat;
But I wouldn't be a postman if…
The walking hurt my feet.
Would you?

C.J. Dennis[32]

Students can choose any occupation, such as a 'firey' (fire brigade), 'ambo' (ambulance), 'copper' (police force), 'chippy' (carpenter), 'sparky' (electrician), 'chalky' (teacher), 'brickie' (bricklayer). I have deliberately used the Australian terms for the various occupations so that the two-syllable word scans and also because it is fun! Retain 'I'd like to be…' as well as the final three lines – with appropriate substitutes for the occupation.

Persona poems

Although young writers will tend to write poems that focus on their lives, it is a good idea to have them write from another person's (or animal's or inanimate object's) point of view. It is also good to write poems that speak for people whose voices cannot be heard. To write a persona poem, a stimulus is needed. You could present students with a drawing, painting or photograph of a person, bird or animal and have the students write in the 'voice' of the other. Alternatively, ask students to bring in photos of their pets. Before writing, ask students to talk about their pets' wishes, needs and opinions.

Shape or 'concrete' poems

Most students (especially visual and spatial learners) are fascinated by shape poems, which capture the eye through the use of imaginative visual images and, often, witty comments. In Sharon Creech's *Love that Dog*, the reaction of the student when first introduced to shape poems reflects the general fascination with them.

My brain was pop-pop-popping
when I was looking at those poems.
I never knew a poet person
could do that funny
kind of thing.
I have tried one of those
Poems that looks like what it's about.

Sharon Creech[33]

Some shape poems make their points instantly, such as S.C. Rigg's 'The Apple' and Max Fatchen's 'Skate Board',[34] whereas others reward long contemplation, such as Alan Ridell's 'Revolver'.

The Apple

```
                              s
                            t
                          e
                        m

              apple  apple        apple apple
            apple yum apple   yum   apple yum apple
          juicy juicy juicy juicy juicy juicy juicy juicy juicy
         crunchy crunchy crunchy crunchy crunchy crunchy
         red yellow green red yellow green red yellow green red
       apple apple apple apple apple apple apple apple apple apple
       apple  apple apple apple apple apple apple apple apple  apple
       apple  apple apple apple apple  apple apple apple apple  apple
       yum delicious  yum delicious yum delicious yum delicious  yum
      yum yum yum yum yum yum yum yum yum yum yum yum yum
      yum yum yum yum yum yum yum yum yum yum yum yum yum
      yum yum yum yum yum yum yum yum yum yum yum yum yum
       yum yum yum yum yum yum wormy worm yuk  yuk  yum yum
       yum yum yum yum yum yum wormy worm  yuk  yuk yum yum
        yum yum yum yum yum yum yum yum yum yum yum yum
         yum delicious yum delicious yum delicious yum delicious
           apple apple apple apple apple apple apple apple apple
            apple apple apple apple apple apple apple apple
              apple apple apple apple apple apple apple
               red yellow green red yellow green red
                crunchy crunchy crunchy crunchy
                  juicy juicy juicy juicy
                     apple apple
```

S.C. Rigg[35]

Revolver

Alan Riddell[36]

Examples of shape poems can be found in many general anthologies but there are also published collections, such as John Foster (1998) *Word Whirls and Other Shape Poems*, Paul B Janeczko (2005) *A Poke in the I* and Andrew Fusek Peters (1999) *The Upside Down Frown*, which has been described by one reviewer as "the funkiest shape poetry ever sandwiched between the covers of a book".

To get your students started writing shape poems, you might like to provide the outline of an everyday object. Ask the students to write a shape poem by inserting descriptive or emotive words they associate with the object inside the outline.

Conversation or dialogue poems

These poems consist of more than one voice but, unlike conversations in a film or play, they usually have poetic elements such as rhyme, rhythm and compression of words. Since they generally reflect the idioms, nuances and cadences of the spoken voice, conversation poems often make use of dialect, phonetic spelling and slang.

In their 'poet's notebook', ask students to jot down conversations (complete or snippets) they have overheard in public, on the bus, in the supermarket, at the beach, in the playground or at a sporting event. Telephone and mobile phone conversations can be turned into excellent poems, particularly as the listener only hears one side of the conversation and has to imagine the response. Although conversation poems are a good way of developing listening skills (and competency in the use of punctuation!), students need to be mindful of their subject's right to privacy when writing their poems, and they will need to find some way around using the swearing that they may hear. Encourage students from non-English speaking backgrounds to use words and phrases from their own languages.

The format of conversation poems can vary considerably. They may consist of questions and answers – separate lines for each or separate stanzas. Before reading 'Studup', you may like to read some examples of Australian idiom from *Let Stalk Strine*.[37] Also, it is essential that students be given a copy of 'Studup' so that they can 'see' the words and appreciate the (British) dialect.

Studup

'*owayer?*'
'*Imokay.*'
'*Gladtwearit.*'
'*Howbowchew?*'
'*Reelygrate.*'
'*Binwaytinlong?*'
'*Longinuff.*'
'*Owlongubinear?*'
'*Boutanour.*'
'*Thinkeelturnup?*'
'*Aventaclue.*'
'*Dewfancyim?*'
'*Sortalykim.*'
'*Wantadrinkorsummat?*'
'*Thanksilestayabit.*'
'*Soocherself.*'
'*Seeyalater.*'
'*Byfernow.*'

Barrie Wade[38]

As a variation, you may ask students to write a conversation between two unlikely companions. Consider the following conversations between imaginary or 'unlikely' friends: an owl and a pussy-cat; a spider and a fly; a walrus and a carpenter; a spider (Charlotte) and a pig (Wilbur); a kangaroo and an emu (on the Australian coat of arms). One of my favourites is the conversation between Archy (a cockroach who was, in another life, a free verse poet) and Mehitabel (an amoral, hedonistic alley cat).[39] Other conversation poems could be between inanimate objects, such as a shoe and a sock, a knife and a fork or thunder and lightning.

Acrostics

I am not a fan of acrostic poems (nor diamentes) and the way they are sometimes used in the classroom. Most of the students' efforts tend to be superficial and by trying so hard to rhyme their lines they produce really trite stuff. I have however, on occasion, been pleasantly surprised with the results! Before writing, it is important to talk to your students about rhyme and free verse and discuss which is most effective for the purpose. Place names work well in acrostic poems and the following class poem from Year 3 at Collarenebri was extremely well received at the school assembly.

Cotton farms, crops and chickpeas
On the banks of the Barwon River
Lures people to fish
Lands of sheep and cattle grazing
Aboriginal name for many flowers
Roos, rabbits and roaming pigs
Emus running free
North east of Walgett in NSW
Endless North west plains
Brown and green lands
Rocky Ford Bridge
It's the place to live!

Year 3 Collarenebri Central School

The students planned their own presentation of this poem to the school assembly. They drew each letter on a large piece of cardboard and imitated a cheer squad. One student called out 'Give us a C', at which two children held up their letter and read the description and so on throughout the entire word. At the end they all jumped up and, with enormous enthusiasm, shouted 'Collarenebri!'. The applause was deafening!

Place names

Australia has some memorable place names and, using a postcode list, students could select a range of interesting ones. Using any poetic form, students can write a poem on any number of them. The following poem by Max Fatchen should get them underway!

Games with Names

Bedgerebong and Kooloonong
Take spelling that's adroit
While Kooweerup you should look up
Be careful with Koroit.
If La Perouse seems better news
Though some prefer Menangle,
A good hard look at Quambatook
May help you sort the tangle.

While Yacandandah's nice verandahs
Surround each pleasant villa
Dandongadale will make me pale –
I'm fine with Cowandilla.
Tangambalanga, Quorrobolong?
Pronouncing them I've tried.
I'll wait until, at Broken Hill,
They get my tongue untied.

Max Fatchen[40]

Encourage students to research the origin of the place name and, where applicable, the Aboriginal meaning. Students from non-English speaking backgrounds might like to write poems about place names in their countries of origin.

SONG LYRICS BASED ON PLACE NAMES

One enjoyable way to link music and poetry is to have students write song lyrics about their towns or municipalities. Begin by playing some well-known 'catchy' songs, such as 'I've Been Everywhere, Man' (Lucky Starr), 'You Don't Call Wagga Wagga, Wagga' (Greg Champion and Jim Haynes), 'On the Road to Gundagai' (traditional) and 'The Newcastle Song' (Bob Hudson). Next, try to track down 'Blacktown Boogie' by Dragon and 'Long Jumping Jeweller (from Lavender Bay)' by The Little River Band.

Sometimes local councils run competitions to find a song that celebrates their area. Ask students to write their own lyrics about their town or municipality, using either a well-known tune or a musical arrangement of their own. Students might like to enter their work in any local competitions.

Models of specific poetic forms

The use of models in poetry writing enables students to experience a variety of poetic forms and styles that are essential when writing formulaic poems. You may wish to begin with short simple structures, such as the limerick, haiku, tanka, cinquain, epitaph before progressing to longer more complex forms, such as odes, elegies, lyrics, ballads and sonnets.

Before writing their own poems, students need to become familiar with the form and its rhythms through listening to a number of examples being read aloud. Also, you may need to model or joint construct one or two with the class.

Limerick

Rhyme and metre are essential to the humour of a limerick. A limerick consists of five lines, where the first, second and fifth lines rhyme as do the third and fourth (aabba). The third and fourth lines are usually shorter. However, since not all poets adhere to this formula, there is no reason why students should have to. The first two of the following limericks follow the traditional formula but the last two do not. It is important to remind students to respect the feelings of their peers and avoid writing offensive limericks about them.

There was an Old Lady whose folly
induced her to sit in a holly;
  Whereupon, by a thorn
  Her dress being torn
She quickly became melancholy.

Edward Lear[41]

A rare old bird is the Pelican,
His beak holds more than his belican.
  He can take in his beak
  Enough food for a week,
I'm darned if I know how the helican!

Dixon Merritt[42]

There was a fat lady from Skye
Who was sure she was going to die,
  But for fear that once dead
  She would not be well-fed,
She gulped down a pig, a cow, a sheep, twelve buns, a seven-
Layer cake, four cups of coffee and a green apple pie.

Anon

There once was a limerick called Steven
whose rhyme scheme was very uneven
it didn't make sense
it wasn't funny
and who'd call a limerick Steven anyway?

Steven Herrick[43]

Haiku

This form originated in Japan. In its traditional form it consisted of three unrhymed lines containing 17 syllables – five in the first line, seven in the second and five in the third. It is marked by its simplicity (single idea or feeling) and is often concerned with nature. With its strong visual imagery, it has been described as a miniature photograph in words. Again there is no need to keep rigidly to the number of syllables in each line. Moira Robinson, for instance, finds it easier to work with two lines of ten syllables and her advice about the need to be flexible should be heeded by all teachers: "The heavens are honestly not going to fall if the first line has three or six syllables instead of five. What does matter is that kids know they only have very limited space in which to create a picture and, therefore, every word is important".[44]

Autumn – even
birds and clouds
look old.

Basho (1644-94)

First Haiku of Spring

    cuck oo cuck oo cuck
oo cuck oo cuck oo cuck oo
    cuck oo cuck oo cuck

Roger McGough[45]

  Summer. Lazy days.
Only the bees seem busy.
  Purple plums ripen.

John Kitching[46]

Tanka

A similar type of Japanese poem is the five-line tanka. The first and third lines usually have five syllables and the others seven, making 31 in all. The original version of the example below was written more than a thousand years ago by Okura, on the death of his little son.

Since he is too young
To know the way, I would plead:
'Pray accept this gift,
O Underworld messenger,
And bear the child pick-a-back.'

Okura

Penny Harter's tanka is a modern example.

Fish guts
stain the rowboat's planks:
by the lake's edge
a child is throwing stones
into the deep.

Penny Harter[47]

Cinquain

The cinquain is an American derivative of the haiku and tanka. It consists of five lines and, in its strict form, has a syllabic count of 2, 4, 6, 8, 2. Again, since not all poets follow the conventions of this form, there is no need to insist that the students do. The cinquain, 'Triad', was written by Adelaine Crapsey, the inventor of this form. Further examples of the cinquain and its variations can be found in Chapter 6.

Triad

These be
Three silent things:
The falling snow ... the hour
Before the dawn ... the mouth of one
Just dead.

Adelaine Crapsey

Epitaph

An epitaph is an inscription carved on a tombstone or written with that context in mind. It usually rhymes and lends itself to imitation and distortion. Students are often attracted to the humour of this form. A visit to a local cemetery will reveal a range of more serious and solemn epitaphs!

Here lies a famous escapologist
Who was buried on the 19th, 20th,
And then again on the 21st June.

Anon[48]

He passed the bobby without a fuss,
And he passed the cart of hay,
He tried to pass a swerving bus,
And then he passed away.

Anon[49]

Miss Spelling's
Exclamation points
Were myriad!!!
She lived on
The margin.
And died.
Period.

J. Patrick Lewis[50]

Riddle

A riddle indirectly describes a person, place, thing or idea. It can be of any length and usually (but does not have to) has a regular rhyming scheme.

This thing all things devours:
Birds, beasts, trees and flowers;
Gnaws iron, bites steel;
Grinds hard stones to meal;
Slays kings, ruins town,
And beats high mountains down.

J.R.R. Tolkien[51]

I fly –
Like a bird,
And buzz –
Like a bee,
Got a tail –
Like a fish,
Got a hop –
Like a flea.

Anon[52]

The beginning of eternity
The end of time and space
The beginning of every end,
The end of every place.

Anon[53]

The answers to the riddles above are: 'time'; 'helicopter'; 'the letter E'.

Ode

Older students can experiment with writing a more complex poetic form, such as an ode. Often written without the constraints of formal structure or rhyme, an ode usually celebrates a person, animal or object. Unlike the elegy which tends to have a mournful tone and is often concerned with death, the ode can be light-hearted and about unlikely objects, such as tennis shoes, game show hosts or pop stars. Although the first ode that probably comes to a teacher's mind is Keats's 'Ode to a Nightingale' they could also use George Wallace's 'Ode to a Sneeze' to illustrate the wide variety of themes used by poets. The following ode, written by a 12-year-old boy, not only celebrates the beauty of the Coorong but, also in the last stanza, reflects on the bleak future of the great Murray River.

A long finger of white sand
Glimmering in the sun.
Littered with skeletons of crabs
And seaweed.
Washed up by the murky sea of salt.
Sand dunes
With tufts of grass.
Prints of emus and kangaroos,
A reminder
Of who lives there.

Standing
On the top of dunes,
Ocean waves in the distance.
The mighty Murray mouth,
Shallow, filled with sand,
A lagoon forming.

Running down the dunes
In huge leaps,
Skidding in the sand.
Seagulls squawking,
Trying to take our bait.

A crab
Holding my line,
Fighting,
Dragged into the net.
Like the Murray,
Lured by Man
Into captivity.
The line to the Coorong
Slowly dying ...

Phillip Stapleton (age 12)[54]

Ballad

Because ballads tend to use simple language and easy-to-follow actions, students
rarely find them difficult to write. Although they vary in structure from couplets to
six-line stanzas, they all tell a dramatic story. Since ballads form such an important
part of Australian literary history, you may wish to begin a writing session by reading
(or singing) some of the following traditional Australian ballads:

- The Wild Colonial Boy' (traditional)[55]
- 'Botany Bay' (traditional)[56]
- 'Click Go the Shears' (traditional).[57]

  Also students should read (or, preferably, have read to them) the following:
- 'The Man from Ironbark' (A.B. Patterson)[58]
- 'The Shearer's Dream' (Henry Lawson)[59]
- 'The Women of the West' (George Essex Evans).[60]

By way of contrast, students can read some more modern ballads, such as Max Fatchen's 'Ballad of a Waterbed',[61] Bill Scott's 'Lazy Jack'[62] and Troy Thompson's 'The Ballad of Sergeant Thompson',[63] which concerns the death of his 'not so squeaky clean' policeman father.

Further Ideas for Poetry Writing

Subscribers to *The Literature Base* will be familiar with Lorraine Marwood's 'Tips for Writing Poetry'. A published poet, she regularly provides a range of interesting ideas to stimulate young writers. You could also use Paul Janeczko's book *Seeing the Blue Between. Advice and Inspiration for Young Poets*, in which 32 renowned poets provide advice and include some of their own poems.[64]

References

1   Frank, M (1995) *If You're Trying to Teach Kids How to Write ... You've Gotta Have this Book.* Incentive Publications Inc. p68.

2   Foster, J (ed) Mackie, C & Stevens, T (ills.) (2003) *101 Favourite Poems.* HarperCollins UK. Reprinted by permission of HarperCollins Publishers Ltd. © Jack Ousbey.

3   Goodfellow, G (1992) *Triggers: Turning Experiences into Poetry.* Wakefield Press in association with AATE, Adelaide.

4   Hughes, T (1967) *Poetry in the Making.* Faber & Faber, London.

5   Crew, G & Smith, C (ill.) (1998) *Troy Thompson's Excellent Peotry Book.* Lothian Books. Reprinted courtesy Lothian Books.

6   Forbes, P (2000) *Scanning the century: The Penguin Book of the Twentieth Century in Poetry.* Penguin Books.

7   Manning, M & O'Neill, J (1994) *New Ways into Poetry.* Oxford University Press.

8   Rosen, M (1989) *Did I Hear You Write?* Scholastic-Tab Publications, Richmond Hill, Ontario.

9   Henri, A, (2001) *Spooky Poems.* Bloomsbury. Reprinted courtesy Bloomsbury Publishing.

10 cited in Courtice, S (1989) *Babies and bathwater: trends in TESOL.* Paper presented at the QATESOL Conference, Brisbane.

11 Harris, R & McFarlane, P (1983) *A Book To Write Poems By.* AATE, Adelaide p84.

12 Herrick, S (1998) *Poetry to the Rescue.* University of Queensland Press. © Steven Herrick. Reprinted with the kind permission of the poet.

13 also in *Poetry to the Rescue*

14 extract from Allen Ahlberg 'Things I have been doing lately' in Ahlberg, A (1989) *Heard it in the Playground.* Viking Kestrel.

15 extract from Shel Silverstein 'Whatif' in Silverstein, S (1981) *A Light in the Attic.* Marion Boyars UK. Reprinted permission Marion Boyars Publishers.

16 Jessie Pope in *T.O.P.P.S – An Anthology of Students' Writing From The Metropolitan East Region* (1980)

17 J. Charles in *T.O.P.P.S – An Anthology of Students' Writing From The Metropolitan East Region* (1980)

18 in Rosen, M (ed.) (1991) *The Kingfisher Book of Children's Poetry.* Kingfisher.

19 in Lanksy, B (ed.) and Carpenter, S (ill.) *No More Homework! No More Tests!* Meadowbrook Press.

20 Herrick, S (1998) *op.cit.*

21 Mitchell, A & Littlewood, V (ill.) (1993) *The Thirteen Secrets of Poetry.* Simon & Schuster.

22 Thiele, C (1985) 'Poetry and the Magic of Words' in McVitty, W (ed.) *Word Magic: Poetry as a shared adventure.* PETA p2.

23 Rosen, M (1989) *op.cit.*

24 *Reading Time: Journal of Children's Book Council of Australia.* 1992: 36; 4 p6-7.

25 in Benton, M & Benton, P (1990) *Double Vision: Reading Paintings ... Reading Poems ... Reading Paintings.* Hodder & Stoughton Educational, London.

26 *ibid.*

27 Edwards, R & Evans, J (2003) *Crow Feathers: An Indigenous Collection of Poems and Images.* Keeaira Press, Qld.

28 Annandale North Public School, Year 6 2004. Reprinted with kind permission. © Julian Pattie 2004.

29 Annandale North Public School, Year 6 2004. Reprinted with kind permission. © Finn Stanaway-Dowse 2004.

30   Creech, S (2001) *Love That Dog*. Bloomsbury. Reprinted courtesy Bloomsbury Publishing.

31   Herrick, S (1992) *Water Bombs*. University of Queensland Press.

32   in Haynes, J (2002) *An Australian Treasury of Popular Verse*. ABC Books.

33   Creech, S (2001) *op.cit*. Reprinted courtesy Bloomsbury Publishing.

34   in Scott-Mitchell, C, Griffith, K (eds.) & Rogers, G (ill.) (2002) *100 Australian poems for children*. Random House, Australia.

35   Creech, S (2001) *op.cit*.

36   Riddell, A (1972) *Eclipse*. Calder & Boyars. Reprinted courtesy Marion Boyars Publishing.

37   Afferbeck Lauder (1981) *Let Stalk Strine*. Ure Smith.

38   in Harvey, A (1995) *He Said, She Said, They Said*. Puffin.

39   Marquis, D (1987) *archy and mehitabel*. Random House.

40   Fatchen, M (1987) *A Paddock of Poems*. Penguin Books, Australia. © Max Fatchen. Reprinted with the kind permission of the poet.

41   in Janeczko, P (ed.) Raschka, C (ill.) (2005) *A Kick In The Head*. Candlewick Press.

42   in Rosen, M (ed.) (1991) *op.cit*.

43   Herrick, S (1997) *My Life, My love, My Lasagne*. University of Queensland Press. © Steven Herrick. Reprinted with the kind permission of the poet.

44   Robinson, M (1989) *Make My Toenails Twinkle*. Longman Cheshire, Melbourne p73.

45   'First Haiku of Spring' by Roger McGough from *Nailing the Shadow* (copyright © Roger McGough 1987) is reproduced by permission of PFD (www.pfd.co.uk) on behalf of Roger McGough.

46   Foster, J (ed) (2003) *op.cit*. Reprinted by permission of HarperCollins Publishers Ltd. © John Kitching.

47   Janeczko, P (ed.) & Raschka, C (ill.) (2005) *op.cit*. © Penny Harter. Reprinted with the kind permission of the poet.

48   in Rosen, M (ed.) (1991) *op.cit*.

49   *ibid*.

50   Janeczko, P (ed.) (2005) *op.cit*. © J. Patrick Lewis. Reprinted with the kind permission of the poet.

51   Tolkien, JRR *The Hobbit*. Allen & Unwin and Houghton Mifflin Co.

52   in Rosen, M (ed.) (1991) *op.cit*.

53   *ibid*.

54   The Taronga Foundation Poetry Prize (2003, 2004) *Poems by Young Australians*. Random House. © Phillip Stapleton. Reprinted with the kind permission of the poet.

55   Robinson, M (ed.) & Smith, C (ill.) (1999) *Waltzing Matilda meets Lazy Jack*. Silverfish p106.

56   Butterss, P & Webby, E (1993) *The Penguin Book of Australian Ballads*. Penguin Books p3.

57   *ibid* p177.

58   Robinson, M (1999) *op.cit*. p60.

59   Robinson, M (1999) *op.cit*. p211.

60   Butterss, P & Webby, E (1993) *op.cit*. p254.

61   Fatchen, M (1987) *op.cit*. p20.

62   Robinson, M (1999) *op.cit*. p20.

63   Crew, G (1998) *op.cit*.

64   Janeczko, P (2002) *Seeing the Blue Between. Advice and Inspiration for Young Poets*. Candlewick Press.

What passing bells
    for those who die as cattle.
        Wilfred Owen.

6

Writing Poetry: Thematic Units

By focusing on themes, these units enable the teacher to cover a wide range of issues and give access to a variety of resources. They address most issues, events and ideas from an Australian perspective, with an emphasis on Australian poetry, art, music, novels and picture books, but some poems from other countries are also included. Although none of the units is age-specific (most can be modified to the meet the needs, abilities and interests of different year groups), there is no doubt that some are better suited to more mature students.

I have trialled many of these units in poetry-writing workshops across schools in NSW and have also used some of them in university tutorials and teacher professional development courses. The time constraints of these workshops have meant that most of the students' writing in this chapter is still in draft stage. Where possible I have used poems that are still in print and can be found in the anthologies listed in the Bibliography. You can also ask students to find sources by putting up a 'Wanted – a poem, song, artwork on…' poster in the classroom rather than hunting them down yourself! Resist, however, the temptation to use resources which may have only a very tenuous link to a particular theme. Although I have provided a few suggestions for integrating some of the themes across other curriculum areas, I strongly urge teachers to focus on the poetry in any follow-up activity and remember that some themes, such as 'Bullying', are useful for the poetry alone.

Colours

There are so many poems written about colours that it is a good theme to use, especially with younger students. Some poets, such as Doug MacLeod, believe that colour poems are overdone in schools and most tend to be 'boring and predictable'. Having judged numerous poetry writing competitions, he comments that "the number of times I'm reminded that *blue* is the colour of the sky makes me wish that overuse of pressure packs will liberate us all by destroying the ozone layer for good. At least the colours will be more interesting!".[1] Writing a definitional poem, however, is relatively easy for young student writers and helps them develop confidence.

Pre-writing activities

- Encourage students to go beyond an obvious description or comparison and exercise their imaginations. E.V. Rieu's 'The Paint Box'[2] with tigers painted in crimson and white, camels in blue and panthers in purple should give them some fresh ideas about colour and the use of it.

- Rather than asking students to write about primary colours, suggest alternatives such as crimson, scarlet, ruby, ultramarine, indigo, azure, chartreuse, emerald, turquoise, olive, amber, ochre, ecru.

- Discuss the language of colours and how they are used to evoke moods (eg. 'I'm in the pink', 'she's in a black mood').

- Discuss the various Australian uses of the word 'blue', for example to describe a red-headed person, an argument or fight, a rude joke, a mood, a type of music, a breed of dog.

- Discuss how colours have a particular meaning or significance associated with certain events or attitudes: red poppies for Armistice Day, green for St Patrick's Day, white feathers for cowardice, yellow ribbons hung on trees to welcome home soldiers, and purple for royalty. Also, look at the Aboriginal flag and discuss the significance of the colours – yellow (sun), black (the colour of skin) and red (the colour of the earth or the bloodshed).

- Decorate your classroom with coloured balloons, streamers or ribbons to stimulate students' talk about how colours make them feel.

- Provide sheets of different coloured cardboard on which the students can write their poems.

- Read a number of 'colour' poems. Since Christina Rossetti's 'What is Pink?' describes so many colours, it is a good place to start.

What Is Pink?

What is pink? A rose is pink
By the fountain's brink.
What is red? A poppy's red
In its barley bed.
What is blue? The sky is blue
Where the clouds float through.
What is white
Sailing in the light.
What is yellow? Pears are yellow,
Rich, ripe and mellow.
What is green? The grass is green,
With small flowers between.
What is violet? Clouds are violet
In the summer twilight.
What is orange? Why, an orange,
Just an orange!

Christina Rossetti[3]

Mary O'Neill, who wrote poems on many colours, including black, white and red, thought that orange meant much more than a piece of fruit.

What Is Orange?

Orange is a tiger lily,
A carrot, A feather from
A parrot,
A flame,
The wildest colour you can name.
Orange is a happy day
Saying good-bye
In a sunset that
Shocks the sky.
Orange is brave
Orange is bold
It's bittersweet
And marigold.
Orange is zip

Orange is dash
The brightest stripe
In a Roman sash.
Orange is an orange
Also a mango
Orange is music
Of the tango.
Orange is the fur
Of the fiery fox,
The brightest crayon in the box.
And in the fall
When the leaves are turning
Orange is the smell
Of a bonfire burning …

Mary O'Neill[4]

'Red' by Aboriginal poet, W. Les Russell, provides a different perspective.

Red

Red is the colour
of my Blood;
of the earth,
of which I am a part;
of the sun as it rises, or sets,
of which I am a part;
of the blood
of the animals,

of which I am a part;
of the flowers, like the waratah,
of the twining pea,
of which I am a part;
of the blood of the tree
of which I am a part.
For all things are a part of me,
and I am a part of them.

W. Les Russell[5]

For something that is guaranteed to delight students, try this extract from 'The Colour Pink', written by Gary Crew in the persona of 12-year-old Troy Thompson.

The Colour Pink

Pink is the colour of my twin cousins' bums
    Of dimples on plums
    Of inside our gums,
And strawberry icecream and other yum yums.

Pink is the colour of the sky right at dawn,
    Of a well-boiled prawn
    Of the mushroom toad's spawn,
And the colour of tonsils before they're withdrawn
        (that's just if you yawn)!

Pink is the colour of icing on cakes
(The sugary mouse sort that my mother bakes),
Of some of the nicest of MacDonald's shakes
And even the rattles on certain cute snakes.

So for the kids who wear black every day and all night
'Cause they think they are Gothic (or some other fright),
You should sit up and take notice of Troy Thompson, your shrink,
Who says, 'Y'only haff livin' if y'ain't wearing pink'.

Gary Crew[6]

Poetry writing

Organise your students in pairs or small groups for a poetry writing activity. Suggest that they write at least four lines (which need not rhyme) on their colour.

Students can so often surprise their teachers. A six-year-old in one of my classes once handed in the line: 'My husband is orange!'. She was absolutely delighted with her contribution. Some other examples of lines written by students in Years 1 to 3 include the following.

- *Red, Red is the colour of the hot planet in the sky.*
- *Grey is a very sad colour.*
- *Green is the colour of asparagus which I hate.*
- *I am black.*
- *Pink is quite nice but it's too luvy dovey.*

A very different and insightful 'colour' poem was written by a nine-year-old boy in 1970, when America and Australia were involved in wars in Vietnam and Cambodia.

Red

Red is the anger of the world
Red is the embarrassment of soldiers when they kill innocent civilians
Red is the blood shed by American students protesting about the sending of troops to war.
Red is the colour of the eyes of families whose loved ones have died in war.

Michael Tunica (aged 9)[7]

Follow-up activities

- Show students *Luke's Way of Looking*[8] and discuss the use of colours.
- Discuss how colour can change our perspective. Compare drawings in black and white or sepia with those in colour. Look at some of Picasso's paintings from his 'blue' period.
- Look at some examples of indigenous art. Discuss the symbolism of colour and style. Although *A is for Aunty*[9] is an alphabet book, the illustrations by the Aboriginal artist/author provide an excellent insight not only into Aboriginal art but also into her experience of growing up on a mission.
- Show students the Aboriginal flag and then read Anita Heiss's poem.

The Koori Flag

There's black for our skin
And what we feel within.
There's yellow for the sun
Giver of life since time began.
Then there's red
To signify our bloodshed.
And there's the meaning of the Koori flag.

Anita Heiss[10]

Food - Glorious Food!

This theme has a universal appeal and the following unit is enjoyed as much by tertiary students as by primary or secondary aged students. Apart from consuming it to satisfy hunger, many of us have used it, at some time, as a pacifier, reward or comfort. The topic of food is inclusive and relevant to all students and may be integrated within a number of key learning areas, such as Creative Arts, Physical Education and Health, and Studies of Society and Its Environment.

Pre-writing activities

- Involve your students in a small group or class discussion on food. What do they like and dislike? Share your own likes and dislikes with them.
  - Compile a blackboard summary of responses. Highlight any vegetables that are universally disliked. If you teach in a school with students from non-English speaking backgrounds you should have a very interesting cross-cultural list.
  - Discuss how our senses can determine what we like/dislike. Although many students have not tasted snails, brains or octopus, often they will include them on their 'don't like' list based solely on the sight of them. They tend to apply the same principle to the smell of food.
- Read aloud some of the following 'food' poems.
  - Frank Flynn, 'Spaghetti'[11]
  - Steven Herrick, 'The Menu'[12]
  - Elizabeth Honey, 'Honey Sandwich'[13]
  - Roger McGough, 'Vegetarians' (see Chapter 2)
  - Lewis Carroll, 'Turtle Soup'
  - June Crebbin, 'Dinner-time Rhyme'
  - Russell Hoban, 'Egg Thoughts'
  - Sidney Hoddes, 'Mashed Potato/Love Poem'
  - Eve Merriam, 'A Matter of Taste'
  - Ogden Nash, 'Celery'
  - Nina Payne, 'Chocolate Cake'
  - Jack Prelutsky, 'Twickham Tweer (Who Ate Uncommon Meals)'
    Many of these poems, which can be found in the Walker, Hutchinson or Collins anthologies (refer to the Bibliography), are humorous.
- Poems such as 'Do You Carrot All for Me?' not only amuse students but also help them to appreciate a poet's imagination.

Do you carrot all for me?
My heart beets for you,
With your turnip nose
And your radish face.
You are a peach.
If we cantaloupe,
Lettuce marry;
Weed make a swell pear.

Trad.[14]

- Follow the poetry sharing sessions by reading from relevant picture books and/
  or some extracts from novels.

Picture books

– Pamela Allen *Brown Bread and Honey*[15]

– Libby Gleeson, illustrated by Armin Greder *The Princess and the
  Perfect Dish*[16]

– Marcia Vaughan, illustrated by Daisy Utemorrah and Pamela Lofts
  Wombat Stew[17]

– Ann Zamorano, illustrated by Julie Vivas *Let's Eat*[18]

Novels

– Lewis Carroll *Alice in Wonderland* (Mad Hatter's Tea Party)

– Jackie French *The Café on Callisto*[19]

– Norman Lindsay *The Magic Pudding*[20] (particularly the last ten pages of the
  first chapter.)

– Pat Lowe *The Girl with No Name*[21] (read pp. 71-79 where Mathew enjoys a
  meal with No Name's Aboriginal family)

– Ruth Starke *Nips XI*[22] (Chapter 23, pp 211-215 the multicultural post-match
  'afternoon tea')

– Further literature resources are given in *The Literature Base* Volume 13, Issue
  2, May 2003.

Preparation for writing

Buy a range of 'unusual' fruit and vegetables. Make sure to include a range of shapes,
forms and colours. The following work well and can be found in most supermarket
food halls or Asian markets: aubergine (eggplant), artichoke, starfruit, tamarillo,
fennel, pitaya (dragon fruit), ginger, coconut, rambutan, bitter melon, kiwano. Before
commencing the activity, check whether any of your students have any allergies or
religious objections to any of the foods.

- Organise the students into groups of four and cover their desks with
  newspaper. Place one piece of fruit or one vegetable on each desk.

- Ask the students to write words that describe what it looks like, smells like, feels like and maybe even sounds like.
- Go around the room and cut the item in half or quarters. The group with the coconut can take it outside and smash it! Ask the students to add to their word list, by comparing what it looks like on the outside to the inside. They can also describe the smell, which is usually more intense when it is opened.
- Invite students to taste the fruit or vegetable and to add words that describe the taste to their word bank. Assure the students that none of the fruit and vegetables will harm them!

Poetry writing

Since the students will be asked to write sensory poems, start by reading to your class Ursula Hourihane's 'My Senses'.

My Senses

Wouldn't it be a dreadful thing
If I hadn't a voice, and couldn't sing?

Supposing I never had a nose
To sniff wet earth or scent a rose?

And oh! If I'd got no eyes to see
The beauty of bird, and flower, and tree!

How sad if I could no more hear
The blackbird's whistle, loud and clear.

And I should miss it, oh so much,
If I'd no feeling in my touch.

Thank You, dear God, for letting me
Feel, Hear and Speak, Taste things and See.

Ursula Hourihane

Students may choose their own poetic form, such as ode, list, conversation (eg between the stomach and certain food), lyric, metaphor and shape poems. A good 'ode' model such as 'Ode to Salted Mutton Birds' by Aboriginal poet Jim Everett can be read to the class.

Ode to Salted Mutton Birds

Mutton birds! I like 'em I'll eat 'em any way.
Skin 'em 'n braise 'em and serve 'em on a tray.
Stuff 'em 'n bake 'em, and serve 'em with sauce.
Or put 'em over the coals, on a spit of course.
I like 'em grilled, I like 'em fried.
And there's plenty other ways I've tried.
But salted birds, just scar and boil.
With carrots, spuds and swedes as well.
It's the best way known to man or beast.
To eat mutton birds and have a feast.

Jim Everett[23]

Poems can be written individually, in pairs or in small groups. Explain to your students that the poems can be serious, comic or sheer nonsense. One Year 4 class at Collarenebri chose to write 'missing title' poems. Leaving out the name of the particular fruit or vegetable, they wrote short, descriptive, sensory poems in free verse. Some of the poems were then read at the school assembly and the audience was asked to guess the title. The students threw them a lolly if they guessed correctly! The 'Aubergine' poem is one example.

Smooth and purple on the outside
Spongy, yellowy and white on the inside
I have no identifiable taste or smell
But if you add tomatoes, onions and spices
I can taste scrumptious.
At times, you'll find me in lasagne
Or a Greek dish called Moussaka.
What am I?

Year 4, Collarenebri Central School

For younger students, you may need to provide a particular poetic form. The five line cinquain (see Chapter 5) works well as it presents a compact image of the item. The following (Australian) variation works well with most students.

Line 1 One word to state the subject
Line 2 Two words to describe the subject
Line 3 Three words to describe the subject
Line 4 Four words about the subject
Line 5 One word to comment on the subject

After a poetry workshop, the following poems were written by students in Years 3 and 4 and were published in the Warrimoo Public School newsletter.

starfruit

bumpy, slippery
green and rough
smells like a watermelon
    sour.

Eden Cottee[24]

tamarillo

  crimson, smooth
  shiny, small, slippery
  it smells like passionf[...]
    bitter

Caleb Smith[25]

kiwano

  hard, cucumber
  tastes like jelly
  like a spiky orange
    yummy.

Jayden Plummer[26]

Follow-up activities

Ask students to write one of the following:

- a list poem on food allergies (eg. 'Fred is allergic to peanut butter/ Tessa can't eat dairy products … I wish I was allergic to brussel sprouts!').
- a group poem on ways to make an unpopular vegetable more palatable.
- an ode to bush tucker.
- a conversation poem between a vegetarian and a selection of fruit and vegetables or a dialogue between a vegetarian and a meat-eater.
- a sensory poem as a response to an excursion to a restaurant with very aromatic food – for example, Greek, Italian, Vietnamese, Lebanese or Indian.
- a descriptive poem about festive food eaten at religious festivals or other occasions that are important for local communities or students.
- a 'recipe' poem about food or another topic, such as love. They could use Jack McGrath's poem on 'Mother Making' as a model.

Mother Making

7 tablespoons of goodness
1 cup of love
9 cups of generosity
a few pinches of sweetness
3 tablespoons of kindness
an ounce of fairness
knowledge chopped finely
3,000,000 cooking skills
a few pieces of acceptance
20 slices of patience
1 cup of fitness.

Preheat the oven to 57 Kalgoorlie Celsius. Mix love and fairness in a bowl, then add great cooking skills followed by knowledge. Stir together well before adding sweetness and pouring in generosity. While still stirring add goodness and kindness. Next sift in fitness and patience. Stir for a few minutes before adding acceptance. Let it set for eighteen years and put it into the oven for six to eight years.

For icing: *Add great cleaning skills to melted dusting skills and add 200 grams of crushed vacuum handling.*

Jack McGrath (age 11)[27]

Curriculum links

The following ideas offer ways to integrate the theme of food across different curriculum areas.

- Ask the students to research the piece of fruit or the vegetable that they used in their 'food' poem (Studies of Society and Environment/ Human Society and Its Environment). The description need only be a paragraph along the lines of the following example.

  Dragon fruit is a type of cactus that originated in South America. The French introduced the plant to Vietnam 100 years ago, where it was initially grown exclusively for the kings and wealthy families. Dragon fruits are delicious eaten as a fresh fruit and make a great addition to a fruit salad. They can be used in any way that a kiwifruit is used. They are grown in Australia in the Northern Territory and north Queensland.

- Using a variety of cookbooks and information texts, such as Beatrice Hollyer's *Let's Eat! Children and Their Food around the World*,[28] have students find recipes from different countries that use these fruits and vegetables in their cooking (Studies of Society and Environment/ Human Society and Its Environment).

- Ask students to prepare a meal, based on one or more of the ingredients. Ask younger children to bring a dish that they have cooked at home with the help of an adult (Physical Education and Health).

- Hold a class debate on 'Immigration changes people's taste in food' (Studies of Society and Environment/ Human Society and Its Environment).

- Get students to keep a diary of the meals (breakfast, lunch and dinner) that they have eaten in a given week. Discuss the different types of meals that students eat. Hopefully, your class is a multicultural one! (Physical Education and Health).

- Using the list of food likes and dislikes (created in an earlier activity), have the students divide the items into 'healthy' food and 'junk' food. Refer to Jackie French's *The Fascinating History of Your Lunch*[29] (Physical Education and Health).

- Ask students to research religious festivals and customs that involve food (eg. Lent when Christians give up certain foods or practices for 40 days preceding Easter, and Ramadan when Muslims fast in daylight hours during the ninth month of the Islamic lunar calendar). Students could investigate other food-related religious customs and rituals, such as kosher food (Jewish) and the avoidance of beef (Hindu) (Studies of Society and Environment/ Human Society and Its Environment).

- Although many people fast for religious reasons, many millions of people in the world are starving. Ask students to consider how can we help? Students may wish to participate in Walk Against Want and/or bring in non-perishable food items to donate to a charitable organisation. Look at the United Nations World Food Program website (www.wfp.org). Invite a speaker from one of the charities that donate to the World Food Program. (Studies of Society and Environment/ Human Society and Its Environment)

Body Parts!

This writing unit demonstrates how poetry can often surprise us and how it can be about anything – the beautiful, the ordinary and the extraordinary. Just as with the unit on 'Food', this unit can be linked into several curriculum areas – Science, Studies of Society and Environment/Human Society and Its Environment, Physical Education and Health, and Creative Arts.

Pre-writing activities

Before students write their own poems on this theme, read them poems such as those below: 'Ears', 'Elbows', and 'Toenails'.

Ears

Have you thought to give three cheers
For the usefulness of ears?
Ears will often bring surprises
Coming in such different sizes.
Ears are crinkled, even folded.
Ears turn pink when you are scolded.
Ears can have the oddest habits
Standing straight on rabbits.
Ears are little tape-recorders
Catching all the family orders,
Words according to your mother,
Go in one ear and out the other.
Each side of your head you'll find them,
Don't forget to wash behind them.
Precious little thanks they'll earn you
Hearing things that don't concern you.

Max Fatchen[30]

Toenails

Toenails are my favourite colour, green
Toenails are a very good source of vitamin C
Toenails are what I throw at my sister
    when she takes too long in the bathroom
Toenails are what I eat
    when Mum forgets to give me lunch money
Toenails have fights with walls, and lose
Toenails make lovely sounds
    when scratched down a chalkboard
Toenails get painted on by my sister
Toenails kiss the dirt
    and sometimes take the dirt home for a bath
Toenails are the knife of a foot
Toenails get caught in the carpet
    and trip you over
Toenails hate shoes, socks,

        and

          falling
rocks!

Steven Herrick[32]

Elbows

The elbow has a certain charm
By being halfway up your arm.
Without it you'd be less than able
But never leave it on the table.

Max Fatchen[31]

Read some other related poems to your class.

- Max Fatchen, 'Lipservice'[33]
- Margaret Hillert, 'About Feet'[34]
- Spike Milligan 'The Eye'[35]
- Mary O'Neill, 'Fingers'[36]
- Jack Prelutsky 'Noses'[37]

Poetry writing

Gather ideas and words about the topic with your students before constructing a group poem. After reading the poems above, one Year 6 class put together a group poem, 'Hands'.

Hands

Hands are black, brown and white
Hands stroke, slap and clap
Hands can harm: hands can heal
Hands make gestures – friendly and rude
Hands wave hello and goodbye
Hands can catch a ball and break a fall
Lift you up or drop you down
Hands give and take
Hands make and break
Hands can hurt and flirt
Hands are for holding each other and strangling your brother
Hands are for fiddling when you are tense
Hands are for touching – my favourite sense.

Annandale North Public School, Year 6 2004

Follow-up activities

Students could write list or group poems on other unusual objects such as walls, grass, traffic lights, thongs or windowsills.

Australians at War

This unit is probably best suited to older primary students. Although when working with this unit I expose students to some 'pro-war' poetry and music, these are, mostly, part of the English experience. Most Australian resources decry the futility of war and bemoan the tragic loss of life. Students can write poems at any point in this unit, responding to the various media or as an individual reflection on war.

Pre-writing activities

- Brainstorm what the students already know about wars. Some students may be refugees and have first-hand experiences of war and may be willing to share them. Do not pressure them if they are unwilling!

- List the main wars in which Australia has been involved: Boer War, World War One, World War Two, Korean War, Vietnam War and Iraq War. As a class, discuss why Australia participated in each of the wars. Where was each war fought? What was our contribution? Was it worth the financial costs and huge loss of life?
  Ask students to discuss their attitudes and feelings towards war. Expect and accept divergent opinions.

- Discuss the significance of Anzac Day to Australians and New Zealanders. Should it still be a national holiday? Ask students to discuss what it means to them (one student replied 'old men and boring speeches').
  Read John Lockyer's *Harry and the Anzac Poppy*.[38]

- Read *My Dog* by John Heffernan and show them Andrew McLean's superb illustrations.[39] Have them look at the sad and frightened faces of the people and the poignant drawing at the end of the story of the young boy waiting for his parents to return from war.

- To really 'see' the horrors of war and to appreciate the reactions of poets and musicians, it is a good idea to begin this unit with visual media such as film and art. Although *Breaker Morant*[40] is a superb film, I usually start with Peter Weir's *Gallipoli*[41] and would now use Tolga Ornek's documentary *Gelibolu – Gallipoli*[42] to give a Turkish perspective as well. The paintings of Will Dyson and H.S. Power provide grim images of the horrors of war.

- The illustrations in the picture book, *In Flanders Field*[43] provide an excellent stimulus for poetry writing. Another picture book that I believe is a 'must' for this unit is Gary Crew's *Memorial*.[44] Gary Crew's evocative text is incredibly moving and Shaun Tan's superb illustrations convey so many overt and covert messages, especially the memories that different generations of one Australian family have of war. The fact that the father has never told his son that he fought in Vietnam because "There are some things you don't want to remember, son…" could be combined with the poem, 'A Slow Disease', and relevant music to form a mini-study of the war in Vietnam and the ways in which it differed from the two world wars.

A Slow Disease

My dad went to Vietnam when he was 19 years old.
I think it bruised his soul. There are some things
The human mind should never have to comprehend, some
*   things the body can never forget.*
He doesn't talk about it. Actually, I guess I never asked.
I hate to imagine his puppy young eyes absorbing all that rain
*   and mud and blood.*
The jungle must have seemed like a slow disease
that would continue to
arrest his and so many other hearts
the rest of their lives.

Jewel Kilcher[45]

- Since some songs about war have such powerful and haunting lyrics, it is a good idea to introduce some of these before moving to the words of the poets. It is important to provide the students with copies of the lyrics when you listen to these songs. Also, since some language may offend it is essential that you listen to the songs before playing them to the class.
    – W.W. Francis, 'Australia Will Be There'[46]
    – Eric Bogle, 'And the Band Played Waltzing Matilda'[47]
    – Eric Bogle, 'No Man's Land'[48]
    – Red Gum, 'I Was Only 19'[49]
    – Midnight Oil, 'US Forces'[50]
    – Ronnie Burns, 'Smiley'[51]
    – Cold Chisel, 'Khe Sanh'[52]

The following songs are from countries other than Australia.

    – Billy Bragg, 'The Price of Oil'[53]
    – Donovan, 'The Universal Soldier'[54]
    – Bob Dylan, 'With God on Our Side'[55]
    – Traditional, 'Johnny, I Hardly Knew Ye'
    – John Lennon, 'Give Peace a Chance'[56]
    – John Lennon, 'Imagine'[57]

- Read some of the following Australian poems with your class. There is at least one for every war! You might like to begin with A.D. Hope's 'Inscription for a War' with its powerful message.

Inscription for a War

Stranger, go tell the Spartans
We died here obedient to their commands
            Inscription at Thermopylae

Linger not, stranger; shed no tear;
Go back to those who sent us here.

We are the young they drafted out
To wars their folly brought about.
Go tell those old men, safe in bed,
We took their orders and are dead.

A.D. Hope[58]

– John Batchelor, 'I Saw a Sad Man in a Field'
– David Campbell, 'My Lai'
– Bruce Dawe, 'The Homecoming'
– C.J. Dennis, 'War' from The Moods of Ginger Mick
– Leon Gellert, 'Anzac Cove' (poet fought at Gallipoli)
– Mary Gilmore, 'Gallipoli'
– John McCrae, 'In Flanders Field'
– Dorothea MacKellar, 'Australia's Men'
– Kenneth Slessor, 'Beach Burial'
– Judith Wright, 'Newsreel'[59]

Some of the most moving poems are those written by our soldiers on active duty as a way of coping with the realities of trench life and the loss of their 'mates'. Indeed, some Australian battalions wrote so many poems that they published their own books of poetry! Patsy Adam-Smith writes in *The Anzacs* that the soldiers did not think of themselves as poets but found "rhymestering a less embarrassing way to record their tears, toils and horrors as well as the jubilation of comradeship".[60] For example, when Australian troops at Gallipoli stripped off their clothes and went for a swim, one Australian soldier, Tom Skeyhill (8th battalion, 1915), reacted to the disapproval of the British commanders by writing the following verse.

We ain't no picture postcards,
Nor studies in black and white:
We don't doll up in evening clothes,
When we go out to fight.

We've forgotten all our manners,
And our talk is full of slang,
For you ain't got time for grammar
When you hear the rifles bang.

The 'eat an' the vermin 'ad drove us
nearly balmy,
So we peeled off all our clobber, and we're
called 'The Naked Army'.

Tom Skeyhill[61]

Although many poems are humorous, others are sad and reflective.

Adieu, the years are a broken song,
And the right grows weak in the strife
    with wrong,
The lilies of love have a crimson stain,
And the old days never will come
    again.
An Australian Soldier[62]

Not only muffled is our tread
    To cheat the foe,
We fear to rouse our honoured dead
    To hear us go.
Sleep sound, old friends – the keenest smart
Which, more than failure, moves the heart,
Is thus to leave you – thus to part,
Comrades, farewell!!
Sgt. AL Guppy[63]

The following poems written by school students not only demonstrate the depth of their feelings about war but also illustrate the writing skills and creativity of young writers.

Political leaders:
With political minds
Political alliances
Political binds.

We don't need destruction
We don't need a fight
Don't leave it to their instructions
They haven't got the right.

All the time and all the money,
All the lives they spend
And it's all for nothing
Leading only to our end!
Lena Dimouska (age 13)[64]

Soldiers and Mice

Soldiers in the front lines,
Mice in a trap,
Somewhat the same,
No claim to fame
Living and dying, it's all the same.
Michael Tunica (age 11)[65]

Monuments of Hiroshima

The roughly estimated ones, who do not fit well
    with death's common phrases
For they are by no means 'eating roots of dandelion'
    or 'pushing up the daisies'.

The more or less anonymous, to whom no human idiom
    can apply
Who neither passed away, or on
    nor 'went before', nor 'vanished with a sigh'.

Little of peace for them to rest in, less of them
    To rest in peace:
Dust to dust a swift transition, ashes to ashes
    with awful ease

Their only monument will be of another's casting –
A TOWER OF PEACE, A HALL OF PEACE, A BRIDGE OF PEACE
    – they might have wished for something lasting
Like a wooden box!

Hany Braidy (age 14)[66]

Poetry writing and follow-up activities

- Explore the role played by animals in the war – horses, known as walers (the Light Horse Brigade), camels (the Imperial Camel Corps) and Simpson and his donkey (at Gallipoli). Since most Australian soldiers had brought their horses from Australia, man and beast forged a special bond and, rather than have their horses sold into 'slavery' at the end of the desert campaign, many troopers shot them. The following poem by Major Hogue reflects the close relationship between man and horse.

I don't think I could stand the thought of my old fancy hack
Just crawling around old Cairo with a 'Gyppo on his back.
Perhaps some English tourist out in Palestine may find
My broken-hearted waler with a wooden plough behind.

No; I think I better shoot him and tell a little lie: –
'He floundered in a wombat hole and then lay down to die,'
May be I'll get court-martialled; but I'm damned if I'm inclined
To go back to Australia and leave my horse behind.

Major O Hogue[67]

- Ask students to write an ode, a persona or a shape poem (see Chapter 5) about one of these horses. Those interested in the horses will be fascinated by the illustrated story by Vashti Farrer and Sue O'Loughlin *Walers Go to War*.[68]
- After reading *Memorial*,[69] ask students to write an epitaph (see Chapter 5) for those who died in the Vietnam War.
- As a whole class, brainstorm the sounds of war – gunfire, bombs, air raid sirens, screams. Having collected a word bank of sound words, have the students write sound poems.
- Organise an excursion to the Australian War Memorial in Canberra. Their education department conducts sessions on Australian war poets, such as Kenneth Slessor and Bruce Dawe, relating it to the Memorial's dioramas and other collections in the galleries. Have the students write words and phrases in their 'poet's notebook' to capture their reactions. These can be turned into a sensory poem.
- Arrange for a war veteran to be interviewed by the class. Ask the students to write up the interview as a dialogue poem.
- Show students some of the recruitment posters from World War One and discuss the language of propaganda. Display some of the cartoons and postcards, particularly those drawn by Norman Lindsay in *The Bulletin*. May Gibbs's patriotic postcards featuring the Gumnut Corps are fascinatingly awful! Have students design a recruitment poster or postcard to attract young men and women into the armed forces. Critically examine any current television recruitment advertisements for the army and navy.
- Discuss the role that women played in the wars – in combat and on the home front. Bruce Beresford's film *Paradise Road*[70] and John Misto's play, *The Shoehorn Sonata*,[71] provide moving images of women's suffering, survival and friendship in Japanese prisoner-of-war camps during World War Two. Read extracts from Jackie French's *Soldier on the Hill*[72] to illustrate the contribution of women at home. Perhaps the class can use the discussion to write a group poem.
- Read selections from *Lines in the Sand, New Writing on War and Peace*, edited by Mary Hoffman and Rhiannon Lassiter.[73] Ask the students to select one poem that they like for their own poetry anthology.
- Read some excerpts from non-fiction books such as Anthony Hill's *Soldier Boy*[74] and Patrick Carlyon's *The Gallipoli Story*[75] and compare them with poems about Gallipoli and the Anzacs. Have students decide which they prefer and why.

Curriculum links

This theme has an obvious link with Studies of Society and Environment/Human Society and Its Environment but can be integrated into other curriculum areas. Although the visual arts, music and, of course, English have all been included, you may also undertake the following activities with your students.

- Hand out copies of a world map and have students colour in the various theatres of war where Australians have fought, looking at topography, climate and land use (Studies of Society and Environment/Human Society and Its Environment).

- Make models and/or dioramas of various war scenes, such as trenches (Design and Technology).

- Research the technology of the weapons of war (Science and Technology).

- Analyse the casualties of various campaigns and work out the percentages of Australians killed and wounded which can then be represented as a graph (Mathematics). To personalise this activity, students could first read 'Light Loss' by J. Le Gay Brereton.

Light Loss

'Our loss was light,' the paper said,
'Compared with damage to the Hun':
She was a widow, and she read
One name upon the list of dead
– Her son – her only son.

J. Le Gay Brereton[76]

- Perform a scene(s) from Alan Seymour's *The One Day of the Year*[77] (Creative Arts).

- Look at the differences between what soldiers ate at home and their war rations (Physical Education and Health).

The Wide Brown Land

Australia has a unique natural environment that regularly endures natural disasters, such as droughts, floods and bushfires. However, since European settlement in 1778, the environment has been threatened by man-made 'disasters', such as urban development, logging of forests and pollution of the air and waterways. Whereas some poets, artists and musicians have focused on the beauty of the natural landscape, others have been deeply affected by the wanton destruction of it. This unit illustrates the wide variety of poetic responses to the Australian environment.

Poems written by primary school students who live in the Murray-Darling Basin are published by the Primary English Teaching Association in annual anthologies of students' work under the *Special Forever* project. They are well worth reading to all students as they provide a first-hand look at this particular environment. I have included some of their poems in the unit and the reading lists.

Pre-writing activities

- Most students will be aware of natural disasters that appear on the television news, so begin with a word association activity. Give them the words 'drought', 'flood' or 'bushfire' and ask them to write down their associations under the headings of 'place', 'colour', 'person', 'animal', 'feeling'. Later, these words can be arranged into a poem.

- Play some 'environmental' music that reflects a particular aspect of the environment in order to create a mood while reading and writing.

- Look at some photographs and artworks of natural and human destruction of the environment. Is a picture really worth a thousand words? Can poets more effectively capture the 'beauty and the terror' in words?

- As a class, compare Aboriginal and European uses of the land. Show/read *Papunya School Book of Country and History*.[78]

- Read poems that illustrate different perspectives and attitudes, such as 'My Country' by Dorothea Mackellar and, to illustrate the spiritual relationship that Aboriginal people have with the land, Hyllus Maris's 'Spiritual Song of the Aborigine'.

Spiritual Song of the Aborigine

I am a child of the Dreamtime People
Part of this Land, like the gnarled gumtree
I am the river, softly singing
Chanting our songs on my way to the sea
My spirit is the dust-devils
Mirages, that dance on the plain
I'm the snow, the wind and the falling rain
I'm part of the rocks and the red desert earth
Red as the blood that flows in my veins
I am eagle, crow and snake that glides
Through the rain-forest that clings to the mountainside
I awakened here when the earth was new
There was emu, wombat, kangaroo
No other man of a different hue
I am this land
And this land is me
I am Australia.

Hyllus Maris[79]

- Discuss the different kinds of Australian environments, such as urban, suburban, rural, wilderness, desert and rainforest. Read poems in class that depict poets' emotional responses to the varying landscape. Compare the idealised view of 'the bush' from some of our early poets with the more 'realistic' view of modern writers.

- Read the following poems and stories.

City environments
- Dorothy Rickards, 'City Song'[80]
- Henry Lawson, 'Over the Ranges and into the West'[81]
- Henry Lawson, 'Clancy of the Overflow'[82]
- Jane Bradley 'I Live up There'[83]
- Hilton, N. and Spudvilas, A. *In My Backyard* – a picture book of the inner city[84]
- Libby Hathorn *Way Home*[85]

Country environments
Look through any of the anthologies of Australian poetry mentioned in the Bibliography for poems that express the Australian countryside, such as:
- A.B. 'Banjo' Paterson, 'Australian Scenery'
- John Shaw Neilson, 'The Winter Sundown'
- Henry Kendall, 'A Mountain Spring'
- George Essex Evans, 'A Medley'
- Kenneth Slessor, 'Country Towns'

– Judith Wright, 'South of my Days'
– Meg Everingham (age 9), 'Rainforest'[86]

In Memory of R.E.H.

Again we climb the mountain spur where sober she-oaks sigh,
To cull a wealth of wattle bloom, and seek the purple vine
That round the rugged ironbarks in velvet circles twine.

Louisa Lawson[87]

Rainforests

Lush and green
Damp and cold
The rainforest geckos and lizards
scooting under the rocks
The cool air making dew drops
from leaf trickles
Fall to the ground
In small puddles
The cool ground under my feet.
Rivers and lakes rushing down
At great speeds
Mysterious like a jungle
Trees and branches looking over
you like spirits from the dead
Frozen in time.

Ross Edwards, Garran Primary School 1994

Drought

– P.J. Hartigan (John O'Brien), 'Said Hanrahan'[88]
– Judith Wright, 'Drought Year'[89]
– Will H. Ogilvie, 'Drought'[90]
– Lorraine Marwood, 'To Solve a Drought'[91]
– Oodgeroo Noonuccal, 'Bwalla the Hunter'[92]
– Cathy Applegate and Dee Huxley *Rain Dance* – a picture book about drought[93]

The Worst Drought

The dam dried up,
The feed ran out.
The cattle were really poor.
They started dying.
Skeletons started appearing.
It has been five years and it still hasn't
rained properly.
I haven't seen a drought like this before.
The bore dried up.
The trees and even the cacti died.
It was so dry we couldn't have a shower.
Then it started to rain heavily.
The dam filled up.
The grass started to grow
It rained for one week.
We nearly couldn't get to school.
It hasn't rained for months now
Will it rain again in this special place?

Kevin Jackson (age 9) Chinchilla State School

Bushfire

– Henry Lawson, 'The Fire at Ross's Farm'[94]
– Kenneth Mackenzie, 'Mountain Bushfire'[95]
– Carrie McAtamney (age 11) 'A Bushfire Blaze'[96]

Flood

– Sarah Talbot (age 11), 'The Flood'[97]
– Michael Hayes (age 11), 'The Day The Murray Flooded'[98]
– Katrina Germein *Big Rain Coming* – a picture book with illustrations by
  Bronwyn Bancroft[99]
– Robert Roennfeldt *Tiddalik: the Frog who caused a flood* – an adaptation of an
  Aboriginal Dreamtime legend[100]

Threats to the Environment

Australian flora and fauna have adapted to survive natural disasters. The real
threats to the Australian environment are caused by humans and their misuse of
the land, over-development, exploitation of natural resources and pollution.

– Richard Edwards, 'Ten Tall Oaktrees'[101]
– Gabrielle Bailey (age 8), 'Blue-Green Algae'[102]
– Jeannie Baker *The Story of Rosy Dock*[103] – also a film produced by
  Film Australia

– Jeannie Baker *Window* – award winning picture book[104]
– Jeannie Baker *Belonging* – a companion book to *Window*[105]
– Tara Egan (age 12), 'Pollution'[106]

Writing activities

- Ask students to write a metaphor poem, such as 'concrete mixers are urban elephants'.
- Model a poem (using other aspects of the environment) on 'I am the Master, the dread King Drought'.[107]
- Ask students to write a persona poem, from the perspective of an animal, fish or bird adversely affected by pollution and land clearing.
- Ask students to select one illustration from Jeannie Baker's wordless picture book *Window* and to write a sensory poem to accompany it.
- Using a ballad as a model, get students to write a ballad about an outback worker such as a drover, shearer, farmer or miner.
- The unique and fragile environment of the Coorong has been widely celebrated by Aboriginal poets such as Leila D. Rankine and Margaret Brusnahan, and non-Aboriginal writers such as Colin Thiele in his books *Swan Song*[108] and *Pannikin and Pinta*.[109] After reading these to your class, have the students write an ode or a haiku to an environment that is special to them in Australia or overseas.
- Ask students to write a 'sound' poem, using words that echo the sounds of a particular environment.
- Using 'To a Litterbug' by Lyndall McNab as a model, ask students to write a poem on preventing pollution such as littering.

To a Litterbug

Friend when you stay and sit and take your ease
By bubbling brook or beach or trees,
Please no traces of your wayside meal,
No crumpled bag, no orange peel,
No Sydney Herald littered on the grass:
Others may view this with distaste, and pass.
Let no one say, and say to your shame,
That all was beauty here ... until you came.

Lyndall McNab[110]

- In pairs, get students to write a dialogue poem between a conservationist and a timber worker, or a cotton farmer and the Murray River.
- Using the acrostic poem 'The Basin' as a model, have students write similar acrostic poems about a particular area of their local environment.

The Basin

The baSin is
becoming unPleasant
because the Environment
is being Clogged up
wIth
blue-green Algae through
to the Lake scheme

Make an eFfort to
help Overcome
The hoRrible
polluting Effects of
this eVer-increasing
hazardous Environmental and
health pRoblem.

Todd Hennessy (age 11) Morgan Street Public School[111]

Follow-up activities

- Read excerpts from the following novels:
  – Leonie Norrington *The Barrumbi Kids*[112]
  – Colin Thiele *Landslide*[113]
  – Mary Steele and Jim Tibor *Blotsville* (Winner of the 2003 Wilderness Society Environment Award) [114]
- Hold a debate on whether Australia should sign international conservation agreements, such as the Kyoto Protocol.

The First Australians

Before beginning any work about Australian Aborigines, you should consult with members of the Aboriginal community. I have gained insights and understandings, not from any textbook or Departmental policies and guidelines, but from interaction with Aboriginal people. Some of my formative experiences have included a visit to an Aboriginal cemetery with an elder, and a day at a local Aboriginal Resource centre where three Aboriginal men (from different tribes) taught me about their art, totems, tools/weapons, languages, music and tucker. I have also been fortunate to have had Aboriginal aides in my poetry writing workshops.

It is important to avoid making assumptions about the background and experiences of Aboriginal students in your class. Many Aboriginal students living in the city have little first-hand knowledge of traditional customs and practices. Also, their skin *may not* be black! Indeed, one young Aboriginal student began her poem 'This is our Land' with the lines: '*I am a young aboriginal./ Though I don't look like one/ I still am!*'.[115]

Pre-writing activities

- Invite an Aboriginal storyteller to your class.
- Read some Dreamtime stories.
- Play some Aboriginal music – traditional and modern. Have Aboriginal speakers and musicians explain the spiritual significance of traditional musical instruments such as the didgeridoo (only played by males) and perform some music to illustrate how the didgeridoo, the clapping of hands and the clapsticks (bilma) are used to echo sounds that occur in the natural environment.
- Have students sing (and dance to) 'Bran Nue Dae'.[116]
- Play some modern rap music performed by young students such as the Wilcannia Mob.[117] Play music by bands such as Yothu Yindi (for example their CD *One Blood*[118]). Discuss some of the political themes that are raised in the songs, such as land rights and reconciliation. Once you have played music from Aboriginal bands, you could also play songs from non-Aboriginal bands, such as Midnight Oil's 'Beds are Burning'.[119]
- Look at a range of Aboriginal art. Books by Christine Nicholls – *Art, History, Place: Indigenous Australian Art*[120] – and Rebecca Edwards and Janelle Evans – *Crow Feathers: An Indigenous Collection of Poems and Images* – provide a useful introduction to Aboriginal art.[121]

- Show the film *Rabbit Proof Fence*[122] and have the students read Anthony Hill & Mark Sofilas *The Burnt Stick*.[123] I make this book a compulsory text for students at university and am always amazed by their reactions – 'I didn't know that this [the stolen generation] happened!'.
- Read poems by Aboriginal people such as those in this unit and listed in the Bibliography.
- As a class, discuss what racism is. Have they observed instances of racism? Point out that skin colour often forms the basis of racism. Read the following poems 'Names', 'Walking Black Home', 'The Colours of Aboriginality' and 'Coloured' about the experience of having a different skin colour, both in Australia and in other countries.

Names

Today my best pal, my number one,
Called me a dirty darkie,
When I wouldn't get her a sweetie.
I said, softly, 'I would never believe
You of all people would say that word to me.
Others, yes, the ones
That are stupid and ignorant, and don't know better, but
Not you, Char Hardy, not you.
I thought I could trust you.
I thought I could trust you.
I thought you were different.
But I must have been mistaken.
Char went a very strange colour.
Said a most peculiar, 'Sorry,'
As if she was swallowing her voice.
Grabbed me, hugged me, begged me
To forgive her. She was crying.
I didn't mean it. I didn't mean it.
I felt the playground sink. Sorry, Sorry.
A sea-saw rocked, crazy, all by itself.
An orange swing swung high on its own.
My voice was as hard as a steel frame;
'Well then, what exactly did you mean?'

Jackie Kay[124]

Walking Black Home

That day waz
A bad day,

I walked for
Many miles,

Unlike me,
I did not

Return any
Smiles.

Tired,
Weak
And
Hungry,

But I would not
Turn
Back,

Sometimes it's hard
To get a taxi
When you're BLACK.

Benjamin Zephaniah[125]

The Colours of Aboriginality

I've been called Vegemite,
And Coco Pop too.
I've been called Chocolate Drop.
I tell you it's true.

The colour of my skin
Is cause for concern
To all those whitefellas
Who simply must learn ...

Anita Heiss[126]

Coloured

When I was born, I was black.
When I grew up, I was black.
When I get hot, I am black.
When I get cold, I am black.
When I get sick, I am black. When I die, I am black.

When you were born, You were pink.
When you grew up, You were white.
When you get hot, You go red.
When you get cold, You go blue.
When you are sick, You go purple.
When you die, You go green.

AND YOU HAVE THE CHEEK TO CALL ME COLOURED!!!

Anon U5Z[127]

- The following poems are concerned with other aspects and issues of Aboriginal life. One is written by an Aboriginal poet ('Reconciliation'), one by an Aboriginal student ('There He Was'), and one by a non-Aboriginal boy ('The Brolga').

Reconciliation

Black fella
White fella
Dark fella
Light fella.

Different outside
Same within
Same blood
Different skin.

Same planet
Same sun
We are many
We are one.

Jill McDougall[128]

There He Was

I saw him in the morning sun;
At 5.15 a.m.
Just standing there
With a spear.

He didn't know
I was watching him,
But I wished he did.

The sun was just rising
As he dived
And took a swim.
This man was still living his tribal ways
And knew nothing of modern times.

This man did not have luxuries
That money can buy;
But what he had
Nobody could take away;
These things were his pride and destiny –
This man is an original Aborigine.

Leanne Boney (age 15)[129]

The Brolga

The didgeridoo lures the brolga to dance
Her body moves gracefully
Like a young gum
Her feet move faster than any warrior's spear
And as the sounds of the rhythm sticks linger
So does the spirit of the dancing brolga.

Michael Tunica (age 11)[130]

- Ask students to read some of the following novels or some extracts.
  – Jackie French *Walking the Boundaries*[131]
  – Jackie French *Rain Stones*[132]
  – Diana Kidd *The Fat and Juicy Place*[133]
  – Pat Lowe *The Girl with No Name*[134]
  – Meme McDonald and Boori Monty Pryor *My Girragundji*[135]
  – Meme McDonald and Boori Monty Pryor *Flytrap*[136]
  – Leonie Norrington *The Barrumbi Kids*[137]

Writing activities

- Ask students to write a poem of a moment when they may have felt 'different' or were excluded from a group.

Bullying

Unfortunately, this theme is frighteningly relevant to many of our school students. Education authorities have recognised the problem and issued policies, guidelines and resource kits, but literature, particularly poetry, is a very powerful way to help students of all ages explore the issue.

Pre-writing activities

- As a class, use brainstorming to create a word bank of words that describe a bully and his/her behaviour.
- Discuss in class the differences between physical and verbal bullying. Add some 'words that hurt' to the word bank.

- Ask students to share personal experiences of being bullied and focus on feelings such as fear, shame, embarrassment and revenge.
- As a class, list the ways to 'deal with' bullies.
- Who bullies? Point out that it is not only school children (boys and girls) who sometimes bully but also authority figures, such as employers, police, politicians, parents and teachers!
- Read the following poems in class. 'Corporal Punishment' by Steven Herrick conveys a powerful message for teachers while 'Back in the Playground Blues', 'Shame' and 'The hurt boy and the birds' capture the feelings of the victims of bullying. Although Jack Prelutsky's 'The New Kid on the Block' is somewhat lighter in tone, it makes a very good point on gender stereotyping – something often overlooked by the general community.

Corporal Punishment

Teachers don't hit any more. No more cane.
No more strap.
It hurts the child.
Teachers try to help children.
I thought of this yesterday
when Mr O'Neill, our PE teacher,
called Peter
an idiot, a fool, a moron,
in front of Class 5W
during basketball practice.
Teachers can't hit any more
but
they can still hurt.

Steven Herrick[138]

Back in the Playground Blues

Dreamed I was in a school playground, I was about four feet high
Yes dreamed I was back in the playground, and standing about four feet high
The playground was three miles long and the playground was five miles wide.

It was broken black tarmac with a high fence all around
Broken black dusty tarmac with a high fence running all around
And it had a special name to it, they called it The Killing Ground.

Got a mother and a father, they're a thousand miles away
The Rulers of the Killing Ground are coming out to play
Everyone thinking who are they going to play with today?

You get it for being Jewish
Get it for being black
Get it for being chicken
Get it for fighting back
You get it for being big and fat
Get it for being small
O those who get it get it and get it
For any damn thing at all

Sometimes they take a beetle, tear off its six legs one by one
Beetle on its black back rocking in the lunchtime sun
But a beetle can't beg for mercy, a beetle's not half the fun.

Heard a deep voice talking, it had that iceberg sound;
'It prepares them for Life' – but I have never found
Any place in my Life that's worse than The Killing Ground.

Adrian Mitchell[139]

Shame

Alone on Monday night, walking away
    from a fight I never had.
I feel lonely walking down the murky lane.
I can't feel my feet prodding along
    the road because I have other
    things to think about.
Why, why was I so terrified
    of somebody who was no bigger than me?
Whose face I'll never forget, his eyes
    pounding into my face.
Whose voice was so sharp and
    clear, that it made me shiver.
I walk away ashamed.

Malcolm Cragg[140]

The Hurt Boy and the Birds

The hurt boy talked to the birds
and fed them the crumbs of his heart.

It was not easy to find the words
for secrets he hid under his skin.
 The hurt boy spoke of a bully's fist
  that made his face a bruised moon –
   his spectacles stamped to ruin.

 It was not easy to find the words
 for things that nightly hissed
 as if his pillow was a hideaway for creepy-crawlies –
 the note sent to the girl he fancied
 held high in mockery.

 But the hurt boy talked to the birds
 and their feathers gave him a welcome –

Their wings taught him new ways to become.

John Agard[141]

The New Kid on the Block

There's a new kid on the block,
 And boy, that kid is tough,
 That new kid punches hard,
 That new kid plays real rough,
 That new kid's big and strong,
  With muscles everywhere,
 That new kid tweaked my arm,
 That new kid pulled my hair.

That new kid likes to fight,
 And picks on all the guys,
That new kid scares me some
(that new kid's twice my size),
That new kid stomped on my toes,
 That new kid swiped my ball,
  That new kid's really bad,
  I don't care for her at all.

Jack Prelutsky[142]

- Perhaps the most powerful poem I have read on this subject is '1945' by
  Geoffrey Summerfield.[143] Deceptively simple in style, its images are so vivid
  that I feel physically sick each time I read it. For this reason, I would tread

warily when using it in the classroom. It begins with English public reaction to the Nazi persecution of the Jews during World War Two, which they claim 'couldn't happen here', and then turns to a school history revision class about the Spanish Inquisition, the murder of the princes in the tower and the deeds of Genghis Khan, and ends with the teacher's claim that 'It couldn't happen now'. However, as the poem reveals, it does happen here and now in schools.

- Read extracts from the following novels that deal with bullying.
  – Brian Caswell *Mike*[144]
  – James Roy *Captain Mack*[145]
  – Susanne Gervay and Cathy Wilcox *I Am Jack*[146]
  – Simon French *Cannily, Cannily*[147]
  – James Moloney *Buzzard Breath and Brains*[148]

Writing activities

- Ask students to write a dialogue poem (see Chapter 5) between a bully and his/her victim.
- In groups or as a whole class, have your students write a list poem on ten ways that a bully can apologise.
- As a class, write a definitional poem describing a bully, such as the following written by a young Pakistani student.

A bully, a person who picks on others weaker,
A bully, who swears and shouts.
A bully, who after his fight, Walks home, his face lit up
… Pleased with himself.

Amber Lone[149]

References

1 MacLeod, D (1985) 'The Poet as a Mental Mathematician' in McVitty, W (ed.) *Word Magic: Poetry as a Shared Adventure*. PETA, Sydney p22.

2 Prelutsky, J (ed.) & Lobel, A (ill.) (1985) *The Walker Book of Poetry for Children*. Walker Books, London.

3 *ibid.*

4 O'Neill, M (1961) *Hailstones and Halibut Bones*. World's Work Ltd.

5 in Gilbert, K (ed.) (1988) *Inside Black Australia – An Anthology of Aboriginal Poetry*. Penguin Australia. Reprinted courtesy Penguin Books Australia Ltd.

6 Crew, G & Smith, C (ill.) (1998) *Troy Thompson's Excellent Peotry Book*. Lothian. Reprinted courtesy Lothian Books.

7 © Michael Tunica. Reprinted with permission.

8 Wheatley, N & Ottley, M (ill.) (1999) *Luke's Way of Looking*. Hodder Children's.

9 Russell, E (2000) *A is for Aunty*. ABC Books.

10 in Reed-Gilbert, K (ed.) (1997) *Message Stick*. IAD Press, Alice Springs. © Anita Heiss. Reprinted courtesy Curtis Brown Australia Pty Ltd.

11 Rosen, M (ed.) (1991) *The Kingfisher Book of Children's Poetry*. Kingfisher.

12 Herrick, S (1998) *Poetry to the Rescue*. University of Queensland Press.

13 Honey, E (1993) *Honey Sandwich*. Allen & Unwin.

14 Agard, J, Nichols, G (eds.) & Wright, A (ill.) (2004) *From Mouth to Mouth: Oral Poems from Around the World*. Walker Books.

15 (2002) Picture Puffin.

16 (1995) Scholastic Australia, Sydney.

17 (2001) Scholastic Australia, Sydney.

18 (1996) Omnibus Books, Sydney.

19 (2001) Koala Books, Sydney.

20 (1999) Australian Children's Classics, Angus & Robertson, Sydney.

21 (1994) Puffin, Melbourne.

22 (2000) Lothian Books, Melbourne.

23 in Gilbert, K (ed.) (1988) *op.cit.* Reprinted courtesy Penguin Books Australia Ltd.

24 Warrimoo Public School, Year 3 2002. © Eden Cottee. Reprinted with permission.

25 Warrimoo Public School, Year 3 2002. © Caleb Smith. Reprinted with permission.

26 Warrimoo Public School, Year 3 2002. © Jayden Plummer. Reprinted with permission.

27 Primary English Teaching Association and Murray-Darling Basin Commission (1996) *Special Together: writing and artwork by children of the Murray-Darling Basin*. PETA Sydney.

28 (2003) Frances Lincoln and Oxfam.

29 (2001) HarperCollins.

30 Fatchen, M (1999) *Songs for My Dog and Other Wry Rhymes*. Wakefield Press. © Max Fatchen. Reprinted by kind permission of the author.

31 *ibid.* © Max Fatchen. Reprinted by kind permission of the author.

32 Herrick, S (1997) *My Life, My Love, My Lasagne*. University of Queensland Press. © Steven Herrick. Reprinted by kind permission of the author.

33 Fatchen, M (1999) *op.cit.*

34 Prelutsky, J (ed.) (1985) *op.cit.*

35 Milligan, S (1989) *Startling Verse for all the Family*. Puffin Books.

36 Prelutsky, J (ed.) (1985) *op.cit*.

37 Prelutsky, J (ed.) Priceman, M (ill.) (1994) *For Laughing Out Loud: Poems to Tickle Your Funnybone*. Red Fox.

38 (1997) Hodder Children's.

39 (2001) Margaret Hamilton Books, Scholastic Australia.

40 Bruce Beresford (1980)

41 (1981)

42 (2005)

43 Jorgensen, N & Harrison-Lever, B (ill.) (2002) *In Flanders Field*. Fremantle Arts Press.

44 (1999) Lothian Books.

45 Kilcher, J (1998) *a night without armor*. HarperCollins, NY p68.

46 Available from National Library of Australia ref: 5434995.

47 *The Gift of Years* (1970) EMI.

48 *ibid*.

49 *Caught in the Act* (1982) Larrikin Records.

50 *Best of Both Worlds* (1982) HMV.

51 *Volume 1: The Local Years* (1969) Festival Mushroom Records.

52 *Cold Chisel* (1978) WEA Records Australia.

53 http://www.peace-not-war.org/Music/BillyBragg/

54 *Universal Soldier* (2001) Polygram International.

55 *Live 1964* (1963) Columbia Records.

56 *Shaved Fish* (1990) Capitol Records.

57 *Imagine* (1990) Capitol Records.

58 Hope, AD (1981) *Antechinus*. HarperCollins Publishers Australia. Reprinted courtesy Curtis Brown Australia Pty Ltd.

59 These can be found in Rosen, M (ed.) (1991) *op.cit.*; Cass, S. et al (eds.) (1971) *We Took Their Orders and Are Dead*. Ure Smith, Sydney; Laird, J.T. (ed.) (1971) *Other Banners – An Anthology of Australian Literature of the First World War*. Australian War Memorial and AGPS, Canberra; Haynes, J. (ed.) (2002) *An Australian Treasury of Popular Verse*. ABC Books.

60 Adam-Smith, P (2002) *The Anzacs*. Penguin Australia p78.

61 Skeyhill, T (1915) *Soldier Songs from Anzac*. The Specialty Press, Melbourne.

62 From the Diary of an Australian Soldier, September 1917 in Gammage, B (1990) *The Broken Years: Australians in the Great War*. Penguin pxviii.

63 From the diary of CQMS AL Guppy 19/12/1915 in Gammage, B *op.cit.* p110.

64 *T.O.P.P.S – An Anthology of Students' Writing From The Metropolitan East Region* (1980)

65 © Michael Tunica. Reprinted with permission.

66 *T.O.P.P.S – An Anthology of Students' Writing From The Metropolitan East Region* (1990)

67 in Gammage, B *op.cit* p138

68 (2001) Anzac Day Commemoration Committee (Qld.)Inc.

69 Crew, G & Tan, S (1999) *Memorial*. Lothian Books, Melbourne.

70 (1997)

71 Misto, J (1996) *The Shoehorn Sonata*. Currency Press, Sydney.

72 (1999) HarperCollins Australia.

73 (2003) Frances Lincoln, London.

74 (2001) Penguin Books, Melbourne.

75 (2003) Penguin Books, Melbourne.

76 Laird, J.T. (ed.) (1971) *Other Banners – An Anthology of Australian Literature of the First World War.* Australian War Memorial and AGPS, Canberra.

77 (1976) Angus and Robertson.

78 Wheatley, N & Searle, K (2001) *Papunya School Book of Country and History.* Allen and Unwin, Sydney.

79 in Gilbert, K (ed.) (1988) *op.cit.* p60. Reprinted courtesy Penguin Books Australia Ltd.

80 in Morrow, R and King, S M (1996) *Beetle Soup.* Scholastic.

81 in Haynes, J. (ed.) (2002) *An Australian Treasury of Popular Verse.* ABC Books.

82 in Gallehawk, J. (ill.) (1991) *Australian Bush Poems.* Axiom.

83 in Scott-Mitchell, C, Griffith, K (eds.) & Rogers, G (ill.) (2002) *100 Australian poems for children.* Random House, Australia.

84 Hilton, N. and Spudvilas, A (ill.) (2001) *In My Backyard – a picture book of the inner city.* Lothian Books.

85 Hathorn, L. and Rogers, G. (ill.) (1994) *Way Home.* Random House Australia.

86 in Primary English Teaching Association and Murray-Darling Basin Commission (1996) *op.cit.*

87 in Meier, J (1995) *The Mountains – A Selection of Classic Australian Poetry with Contemporary Australian Photography.* Angus & Robertson.

88 Robinson, M (ed.) & Smith, C (ill.) (1999) *Waltzing Matilda meets Lazy Jack.* Silverfish.

89 Wright, J (1994) *Collected Poems: 1942-1985.* Angus & Robertson.

90 *A Treasury of Favourite Australian Poems.* Viking O'Neill, Melbourne.

91 Scott-Mitchell, C, Griffith, K (eds.) (2002) *op.cit.*

92 *ibid.*

93 Applegate, C & Huxley, D (ill.) (2000) *Rain Dance.* Margaret Hamilton.

94 Robinson, M. and Smith, C. *op.cit.*

95 (1961) *The Poems of Kenneth Mackenzie.*

96 Primary English Teaching Association and Murray-Darling Basin Commission (1994) *Portraits of our Land: writing and artwork by children of the Murray-Darling Basin.* PETA Sydney.

97 Primary English Teaching Association and Murray-Darling Basin Commission (1997) *Links with the Land: writing and artwork by children of the Murray-Darling Basin.* PETA Sydney.

98 *ibid.*

99 (1999) Roland Harvey Books.

100 (1980) Penguin.

101 Sage, A (ed) (1998) *The Hutchinson Treasury of Children's Poetry.* Hutchinson Children's Books, Random House UK.

102 Primary English Teaching Association and Murray-Darling Basin Commission (1997) *op.cit.*

103 (1995) Random House.

104 (1991) Random House UK.

105 (2004) Walker Books.

106 Primary English Teaching Association and Murray-Darling Basin Commission (1997) *op.cit.*

107 from WH Ogilvie's 'Drought' in *A Treasury of Favourite Australian Poems.* Viking O'Neill, Melbourne.

108 Thiele, C (2002) *Swan Song.* Lothian Books.

109 Thiele, C & Gouldthorpe, P (ill.) (2000) *Pannikin and Pinta.* Lothian Books.

110 *Youth Writes.* Reed Book Pty Ltd & Longman Cheshire Pty Ltd.

111 Primary English Teaching Association and Murray-Darling Basin Commission (1994) *op.cit.*

112 (2002) Omnibus Books.

113 (1997) Lothian Books.

114 (2002) Hyland House Publishing.

115 Dimitra Vassios in *T.O.P.P.S - An Anthology of Students' Writing From The Metropolitan East Region* (1980)

116 Sound recording: Jimmy Chi *Bran Nue Dae*. Polygram. Playscript and song scores: Jimmy Chi and Kuckles (1991) *Bran Nue Dae*. Currency Press & Magabala Books. Film: directed by Tom Zubrycki (1991) *Bran Nue Dae*. Ronin Films.

117 *Homebake No. 6*. EMI.

118 (1999) Mushroom Records.

119 *Diesel and Dust* (1987) CBS.

120 (2003) Working Title Press, Adelaide.

121 Edwards, R & Evans, J (2003) *Crow Feathers: An Indigenous Collection of Poems and Images*. Keeaira Press, Qld.

122 Phillip Noyce (2002) Miramax Films.

123 Hill, A & Sofilas, M (ill.) (1996) *The Burnt Stick*. Puffin Books.

124 Kay, J (1994) *Three has gone*. Blackie. Reprinted by kind permission of the author.

125 Zephaniah, B. (1996) *Funky Chickens*. Viking. Reprinted courtesy Penguin UK.

126 in Reed-Gilbert, K (ed.) (1997) *op.cit.* © Anita Heiss. Reprinted courtesy Curtis Brown Australia Pty Ltd.

127 in Elkin, J & Duncan, C (eds.) (1995) *Free My Mind*. Puffin Books.

128 McDougall, J & Taylor, J (2000) *Anna the Goanna and other poems*. Aboriginal Studies Press, Canberra. Reprinted by kind permission of the author.

129 *T.O.P.P.S - An Anthology of Students' Writing From The Metropolitan East Region* (1986)

130 © Michael Tunica. Reprinted with permission.

131 French, J & Bancroft, B (ill.) (1993) *Walking the Boundaries*. Angus & Robertson, Sydney.

132 (1991) Angus & Robertson, Sydney.

133 Kidd, D & Bancroft, B (ill.) (1992) *The Fat and Juicy Place*. Angus & Robertson, Sydney.

134 (1994) Puffin Books, Melbourne.

135 (1998) Allen & Unwin, Sydney.

136 (2002) Allen & Unwin, Sydney.

137 (2002) Omnibus Books, SA.

138 Herrick, S (1997) *op.cit.* © Steven Herrick. Reprinted by kind permission of the author.

139 Mitchell, A. (1982) *For Beauty Douglas: Collected Poems 1953-79*. Allison & Busby.

140 Monahan, S (1990) *Life and Laughter: An Active Poetry Book*. Longman Cheshire, Melbourne.

141 Agard, J (1996) *Get Back Pimple*. Viking.

142 Prelutsky, J (1984) *The New Kid on the Block*. Greenwillow.

143 Mitchell, A (ed.) (1996) *The Orchard Book of Poems*. Orchard Books.

144 (1993) University of Queensland Press.

145 (1999) University of Queensland Press.

146 (2000) HarperCollins Sydney.

147 (1981) Angus & Robertson, Sydney.

148 (1998) University of Queensland Press.

149 Lone, A *A bully and his victim*. Placer Publishers. Reprinted by kind permission of the author.

References and Further Reading

Abbs, P & Richardson, J (1990) *The Forms of Poetry – A Practical Guide*. Cambridge University Press.

Adam-Smith, P (1978) *The Anzacs*. Thomas Nelson.

Allen, J & Angelotti, M (1982) 'Responding to Poetry'. *New Essays in the Teaching of Literature. Proceedings of the Literature Commission Third Internationl Conference on the Teaching of English, Sydney Australia 1980*. Australian Association of Teaching English.

Auden, WH (1973) 'How can I tell what I think till I see what I say', in Bagnall, N (ed.). *New Movements in the Study and Teaching of English*. Temple Smith, London.

Auden, WH (1953) introduction to de la Mare, W *Come Hither: A Collection of Rhymes and Poems for the Young of all Ages*. Faber & Faber.

Bennett, J & Chambers, A (1984) *Poetry for Children: A Signal Bookguide*. Thimble Press.

Benton, M & Benton, P (1990) *Double Vision: Reading Paintings … Reading Poems … Reading Paintings*. Hodder & Stoughton Educational, London.

Benton, M & Fox, G (1985) *Teaching Literature: Nine to Fourteen*. Oxford University Press.

Blackie, P (1971) 'Asking questions'. *English in Education*; 5: 3.

Britton, J (1993) *Literature in Its Place*. Cassell Educational, London.

Britton, J (1983) 'Reading and writing poetry' in Arnold, R (ed.) *Timely Voices: English Teaching in the Eighties*. Oxford University Press, Melbourne.

Causley, C (1995) *see* Merrick, B (1995).

Causley, C (1985) 'Poetry and the child' in McVitty, W (ed.) *Word Magic: Poetry as a Shared Adventure*. PETA, Sydney.

Chambers, A (1994) *Tell Me: Children, Reading and Talk*. PETA in association with Thimble Press, Sydney.

Chambers, A (1992) *The Reading Environment*. PETA in association with Thimble Press, Sydney.

Chambers, A (1985) 'Inside Poetry: A Shared Adventure' in McVitty, W (ed.) *Word Magic: Poetry as a Shared Adventure*. PETA, Sydney.

Courtice, S (1989) *Babies and bathwater: trends in TESOL*. Paper presented at the QATESOL Conference, Brisbane.

Duffy, M (ed.) (2000) *A Return to Poetry 2000. Ten Australians choose ten of their favourite poems*. Duffy & Snellgrove.

Ewing, R, Simons, J & Hertzberg, M (2004) *Beyond the Script: Drama in the Classroom*. PETA, Sydney.

Fatchen, M (1985) 'A Verse Along the Way' in McVitty, W (ed.) *Word Magic: Poetry as a Shared Adventure*. PETA, Sydney.

Fox, G (1992) Paper presented at the ARA National Conference, Hobart.

Fox, G & Merrick, B (1983) 'Thirty-six things to do with a poem', in Mallick, D & Jenkins, G (eds), *Poetry in the Classroom*. St Clair Press, Sydney.

Frank, M (1995) *If You're Trying to Teach Kids How to Write … You've Gotta Have this Book*. Incentive Publications Inc.

Fuller, R (1976) 'The influence of children on books'. *Children's Literature in Education*:20.

Gammage, B (1990) *The Broken Years: Australians in the Great War*. Penguin.

Goodfellow, G (1992) *Triggers: Turning Experiences into Poetry*. Wakefield Press in association with AATE, Adelaide.

Hall, L (1989) *Poetry for Life: A Practical Guide to Teaching Poetry in the Primary School*. Cassell Educational, London.

Harding, D W (1976) *Words into Rhythm*. Cambridge University Press.

Harris, R & McFarlane, P (1983) *A Book To Write Poems By*. AATE, Adelaide.

Hayhoe, M (1992) 'Poetry and politics', in Thomson, J (ed.), *Reconstructing Literature Teaching*. AATE, Adelaide.

Johnson, T & Louis, D (1985) *Bringing It All Together*. Methuen, Sydney.

Lysenko, M (1990) 'Poetry in the classroom'. *Reading Time*:34; 2.

MacLeod, D (1985) 'The Poet as a Mental Mathematician' in McVitty, W (ed.) *Word Magic: Poetry as a Shared Adventure*. PETA, Sydney.

Mallick, D & Jenkins, G (1983) *Poetry in the Classroom*. St Clair Press, Sydney.

Manning, M & O'Neill, J (1994) *New Ways into Poetry*. Oxford University Press.

Martin, N (1983) *Mostly about Writing*. Boynton/Cook, Upper Montclair, NJ.

McConnell, R (1991) *Poetry, Poets, and Poetry Teachers*. NZCER and ACER, Melbourne.

McGillis, R (1984) 'Calling a voice out of silence: hearing what we read'. *Children's Literature in Education*:52.

McKay, G (1986) 'Poetry and the young child'. *English in Australia*:75.

McKay, G (1985) 'Teaching poetry as a language'. *English in Australia*:74.

McVitty, W (ed.) (1985) *Word Magic: Poetry as a Shared Adventure*. PETA, Sydney.

Meek, M (1988) *How Texts Teach What Readers Learn*. Thimble Press.

Merrick, B (1995) 'With a straight eye: an interview with Charles Causley', in Fox, G (ed.) *Celebrating 'Children's Literature in Education'*. Hodder & Stoughton Educational, London (originally published in no. 70, 1988) p88.

Monahan, S (1991) *Multivoice Magic: Poetry as Shared Reading*. Longman Cheshire, Melbourne.

Monahan, S (1990) *Life and Laughter: An Active Poetry Book*. Longman Cheshire, Melbourne.

Monahan, S (1988) 'Performing Australian poetry', in O'Sullivan, C (ed.), *Australian Literature in the Primary Classroom*. Curriculum Development Centre, Canberra.

Monahan, S (1985) 'Poetry and Performance 2: children as performers' in McVitty, W (ed.) *Word Magic: Poetry as a Shared Adventure*. PETA, Sydney.

Murison Travers, M (1983) 'Poetry teaching: past and present' in *English in Australia*: 64.

Pradl, G M (ed.) (1982) *Prospect and Retrospect: Selected Essays of James Britton*. Boynton/Cook, Montclair, NJ.

Reeves, J (1959) *Teaching Poetry*. Heinemann, London.

Rehn, R (1992) 'Reading and Writing Poetry' in Thomson, J (ed.) *Reconstructing Literature Teaching*. AATE, Adelaide.

Robinson, M (1989) *Make My Toenails Twinkle*. Longman Cheshire, Melbourne.

Robinson, M (1985) 'How not to "Teach" Poetry' in McVitty, W (ed.) *Word Magic: Poetry as a shared adventure*. PETA.

Robinson, M (1984) *Children's Playground Rhymes, Chants and Traditional Verse*. Primary English Notes, PETA, Sydney.

Rosen, M (1989) *Did I Hear You Write?* Scholastic-Tab Publications, Richmond Hill, Ontario.

Scannell, V (1995) 'Poetry for children', in Fox, G (ed.) *Celebrating 'Children's Literature in Education'*. Hodder & Stoughton Educational, London (originally published in no. 67, 1988) p97.

Scott, B (1996) *Pelicans and Chihuahuas and other Urban Legends*. University of Queensland Press.

Scott, D (1981) *Poetry Is …* Heinemann Educational, Melbourne.

Smith, S (1985) *Inside Poetry*. Pitman Publishing, Melbourne.

Stibbs, A (1981) 'Poetry in the classroom'. *Children's Literature in Education*:40.

Strong, L A G (1946) 'Poetry in school', in da Sola Pinto, V (ed.) *The Teaching of English in Schools: A Symposium*. Macmillan, London.

Summerfield, G (1983) 'Poetry and performance: a lesson', in Mallick, D & Jenkins, G (eds.) *Poetry in the Classroom*. St Clair Press, Sydney.

Thiele, C (1985) 'Poetry and the Magic of Words' in McVitty, W (ed.) *Word Magic: Poetry as a shared adventure*. PETA.

Tucker, N (1973) 'Why nursery rhymes?', in Haviland, V (ed.) *Children and Literature: Views and Reviews*. Scott, Foresman & Co., Glenview, IL.

Watson, K (1981) *English Teaching in Perspective*. St Clair Press, Sydney.

White, E B (1973) 'On writing for children', in Haviland, V (ed.) *Children and Literature: Views and Reviews*. Scott, Foresman & Co., Glenview, IL.

Wilner, I (1979) 'Making poetry happen: birth of a poetry troupe'. *Children's Literature in Education*:10;2.

Wright, J (1966) 'The Role of Poetry in Education'. *English in Australia*; June:2.

Select Bibliography

This is a listing of poetry books that I have referred to in the text, as well as others that you will find useful. Most of the titles are currently in print (almost all are available in paperback editions), and the few exceptions are likely to be found on library shelves. If not, you can locate and buy many of them through the internet. Inevitably there is some overlap between the categories into which the titles have been divided and some books could have found a place in more than one category.

The lists contain a fair proportion of Australian material and some books of multi-ethnic poetry. However, the recommendations are by no means exhaustive, and I apologise if some of your favourites have been omitted.

TREASURIES

Nettell, S (ed.) & Dann, P (ill.) (1995) *Collins Treasury of Poetry*. HarperCollins, London.

Prelutsky, J (ed.) & Lobel, A (ill.) (1985) *The Walker Book of Poetry for Children*. Walker Books, London.

Sage, A (ed) (1998) *The Hutchinson Treasury of Children's Poetry*. Hutchinson Children's Books, Random House UK.

A Treasury of Favourite Australian Poems. (1991) Claremont Books, Victoria.

GENERAL ANTHOLOGIES

Berry, J (ed.) & Lucas, K (ill.) (2001) *Around the World in Eighty Poems*. Macmillan.

Foster, J (ed) Mackie, C & Stevens, T (ills.) (2003) *101 Favourite Poems*. HarperCollins UK.

Foster, J (2000) *Climb aboard the poetry plane*. Oxford University Press.

Hill, S & Strauss, D (ill.) (1991) *Poems Not To Be Missed*. Era Publications.

Ireson, B (ed.) (1970) *The Young Puffin Book of Verse*. Puffin Books.

Kroll, J (1995) *Swamp Soup and other poems*. Lothian.

McFarlane P & Temple, L (eds.) (1998) *Among Ants Between Bees*. Macmillan.

Mitchell, A (ed.) (2001) *A Poem a Day Helps You Stop Work and Play*. Orchard Books.

Mitchell, A (ed.) (1996) *The Orchard Book of Poems*. Orchard Books.

Morrow, R and King, S M (1996) *Beetle Soup*. Scholastic.

Patten, B (ed.) (1999) *The Puffin Book of Utterly Brilliant Poetry*. Puffin Books.

Rosen, M (ed.) (2001) *The Walker Book of Classic Poetry and Poets*. Walker Books USA.

Rosen, M (ed.) (1991) *The Kingfisher Book of Children's Poetry*. Kingfisher.

Rosen, M (ed.) (1987) *A Spider Bought a Bicycle and other poems for young children*. Kingfisher.

Rosen, M (ed.) & Blake, Q (ill.) (2004) *Michael Rosen's Sad Book*. Walker.

Rumble, A (ed.) & Dann, P (ill.) (1989) *Is A Caterpillar Ticklish?* Puffin Books.

Scott-Mitchell, C, Griffith, K (eds.) & Rogers, G (ill.) (2002) *100 Australian poems for children*. Random House, Australia.

SINGLE POET COLLECTIONS

Bell, A (2004) *Muster Me a Song: The Anne Bell reciter*. Triple D Books.

Causley, C & Payne, L (ill.) (1994) *Going to the Fair – Selected poems for Children*. Puffin Books.

Fatchen, M (1999) *Songs for My Dog and Other Wry Rhymes*. Wakefield Press.

Fatchen, M (1989) *A Pocketful of Rhymes*. Omnibus/Puffin.

Fatchen, M (1987) *A Paddock of Poems*. Penguin Books, Australia.

Fatchen, M & Booth, C (ill.) (2003) *Poetry AllSorts: The Max Fatchen Reciter*. Triple D Books.

Fatchen, M & Johns, C (ill.) (2004) *Meet the Monsters*. Scholastic.

Herrick, S (1998) *Poetry to the Rescue*. University of Queensland Press.

Herrick, S (1997) *My Life, My Love, My Lasagne*. University of Queensland Press.

Herrick, S (1992) *Water Bombs*. University of Queensland Press.

Herrick, S & Gorman, J (ill.) (2001) *Love Poems and Leg Spinners. A month in the life of Class 5b*. University of Queensland Press.

Honey, E (1998) *Mongrel Doggerel*. Allen & Unwin.

Honey, E (1993) *Honey Sandwich*. Allen & Unwin.

Kay, J & Tourret, S (ill.) (1994) *Two's Company*. Puffin Books.

MacLeod, D & Smith, C (ill.) (2004) *Spiky, Spunky, My Pet Monkey*. Puffin.

Magee, W & Broadley, L (ill.) (2000) *The phantom's fang-tastic show* Oxford University Press.

Maynard, J (ed.) & Garns, A (ill.) (2003) *Alfred, Lord Tennyson – Poems for Young People*. Sterling Publishing.

McCord, D (1966) *All Day Long. Fifty Rhymes of the Never Was and Always Is*. Little, Brown and Company.

Mole, J (1994) *Back By Midnight*. Puffin.

Reeves, J & Ardizzone, E (ill.) (1987) *The Wandering Moon and Other Poems*. Puffin Books.

Scott, B (2002) *See what I've got: The Bill Scott Reciter*. Triple D Books.

Scott, B (1989) *Following the Gold*. Omnibus/Puffin.

Thiele, C (2003) *Sun Warm Memories:The Colin Thiele Reciter*. Triple D Books.

Thiele, C (1989) *Poems in my luggage*. Puffin Australia.

Zephaniah, B (1995) *Talking Turkeys*. Puffin Books.

THEMATIC COLLECTIONS

Alborough, J (2001) *Guess What Happened at School Today*. HarperCollins, London.

Bradman, T (ed.) & Blundell, T (ill.) (1993) *A Stack of Story Poems*. Corgi Books.

Cass, S, Cheney, R, Malouf, D & Wilding M (1971) *We took their orders and are dead: An Anti-war Anthology*. Ure Smith, Sydney, NSW.

Covernton, J & Smith, C (ill.) (1991) *Putrid Poems*. Omnibus.

Fisher, R (ed.) (1986) *Funny Folk. Poems about people*. Faber.

Fisher, R & Widdowson, K (ill.) (1994) *Minibeasts*. Faber.

Foster, J (ed.) (1998) *School's Out. Poems about School*. Oxford University Press.

Foster, J (ed.) (1993) *All in the Family*. Oxford University Press.

Foster, J (ed.) & Korky, P (ill.) (2000) *Pet Poems*. Oxford University Press.

Gibbs, S (ed.) (2003) *Poems to Freak out your Teacher*. Oxford University Press.

Gowar, M & Buchanan, G (ill.) (1994) *Carnival of the Animals*. Puffin Books.

Henri, A & Smith, W (ill.) (2001) *Spooky Poems*. Bloomsbury.

Hillyer, B (ed.) & Swain, H (ill.) (2003) *Haven't You Grown! Poems about Families*. Jubilee Books.

Janeczko, PB (ed.) & Davenier, C (ill.) (1999) *Very Best (Almost) Friends: Poems of Friendship*. Walker Books.

Lear, E & Harrison, M (ill.) (1998) *Bisky Bats and Pussy Cats*. Bloomsbury.

MacLeod, D & Smith, C (ill.) (2002) *On the Cards*. Puffin.

Marwood, L (2002) *Redback Mansion*. Five Islands Press.

Owen, G (1985) *Song of the City*. Harper Collins.

Nichols, G & Willey, W (ill.) (2000) *The Poet Cat*. Bloomsbury Children's Books.

Prelutsky, J & Sis, P (ill.) (1996) *Monday's Troll*. Greenwillow Books.

Prelutsky, J & Sis, P (ill.) (1993) *The Dragons Are Singing Tonight*. Greenwillow Books.

Scannell, V & Ross, T (ill.) (1992) *On Your Cycle Michael*. Red Fox.

Wolf, A & Clarke, G (ill.) (2003) *The Blood-Hungry Spleen and Other Poems About our Parts*. Candlewick Press.

SINGLE ILLUSTRATED POEMS

Carroll, L & Stewart, J (ill.) (2004) *Jabberwocky*. Walker Books.

Dennis, CJ & Gouldthorpe, PJ (ill.) (1995) *Hist!* Puffin, Victoria.

Frost, R & Jeffers, S (ill.) (2001) *Stopping by Woods on a Snowy Evening*. Dutton Children's Books NY.

Lear, E & Beck, I (ill.) (2002) *The Jumblies*. Corgi.

Lear, E & Beck, I (ill.) (1995) *The Owl and the Pussy-Cat*. Corgi.

Lear, E & Voce, L (ill.) (2005) *The Quangle Wangle's Hat*. Walker.

Noyes, A & Keeping, C (ill.) (1981) *The Highwayman*. Oxford University Press.

Paterson, A.B. 'Banjo' & Blackwood, F (ill.) (2004) *The Man from Snowy River*. Scholastic.

Paterson, A.B. 'Banjo' & Niland, K (ill.) (2002) *Clancy of the Overflow*. Scholastic.

Tennyson, Alfred, Lord & Keeping, C (ill.) (1986) *The Lady of Shalott*. Oxford University Press.

COMIC AND NONSENSE VERSE

Blake, Q (1996) *The Penguin Book of Nonsense Verse*. Puffin Poetry.

Carroll, L & Hussey, L (ill.) (2002) *Nonsense Verse*. Bloomsbury Children's Classics.

Dahl, R & Blake, Q (ill.) (1990) *Rhyme Stew*. Penguin Books.

Dahl, R & Blake, Q (ill.) (1986) *Dirty Beasts*. Puffin Books.

Dahl, R & Blake, Q (ill.) (1984) *Revolting Rhymes*. Puffin Books.

Dugan, M, MacLeod, D (eds.) & Viska, P (ill.) (1993) *Out to Lunch*. Moondrake.

MacLeod, D (2004) *Spiky, Spunky, My Pet Monkey*. Puffin.

MacLeod, D (2002) *Sister Madge's Book of Nuns: Special bumper edition with extra nuns!* Puffin.

MacLeod, D (1981) *In the Garden of Badthings*. Kestrel/Picture Puffin.

MacLeod, D & Brierley, J (ill.) (1984) *The Fed Up Family Album*. Puffin Books.

MacLeod, D & Smith, C (ill.) (1986) *Sister Madge's Book of Nuns*. Omnibus.

McGough, R (ed.) & Holden, C (ill.) (1991) *The Kingfisher Book of Comic Verse*. Kingfisher.

McNaughton, C (1989) *There's An Awful Lot Of Weirdos In Our Neighbourhood*. Walker Books.

Milligan, S (2000) *Silly Verse for Kids*. Puffin. ABC Books.

Milligan, S (1989) *Startling Verse for all the Family*. Puffin Books.

Prelutsky, J (ed.) & Priceman, M (ill.) (1994) *For Laughing Out Loud: Poems to Tickle Your Funnybone*. Red Fox.

Weld, A & Smith, C (ill.) (1990) *Fractured Fairytales & Ruptured Rhymes*. Omnibus/Puffin.

Wright, K (ed.) & Foreman, M (ill.) (1993) *Funny Bunch*. Viking.

SHAPE/CONCRETE POETRY

Foster, J (ed.) (1998) *Word Whirls and other shape poems*. Oxford University Press.

Janeczko, PB (2001) *A Poke in the I – A collection of Concrete Poems*. Walker Books.

Peters, AF (ed.) (1999) *The Upside Down Frown*. Wayland.

ABORIGINAL POETRY

Edwards, R & Evans, J (2003) *Crow Feathers: An Indigenous Collection of Poems and Images*. Keeaira Press, Qld.

Gilbert, K (1988) *Inside Black Australia. An Anthology of Australian Poetry*. Penguin Books Australia.

Gilbert, K (1982) *Child's Dreaming*. Hyland House.

Mafi-Williams, L (ed.) (1993) *Spirit Song. A collection of Aboriginal Poetry*. Omnibus.

Reed-Gilbert, K (ed.) (1997) *Message Stick. Contemporary Aboriginal Writing*. Jukurrpa Books.

MULTICULTURAL POETRY

Agard, J, Nichols, G (eds.) & Felstead, C et al (ills.) (2002) *Under the Moon & Over the Sea: A Collection of Caribbean Poems*. Walker Books.

Charles, F & Toft, L (ill.) (1991) *The Kiskadee Queen. A Collection of Black Nursery Verse*. Puffin.

Elkin, J & Duncan, C (eds.) (1995) *Free my Mind. An Anthology of Black and Asian Poetry*. Puffin Books.

Styles, M (ed.). (1986) *You'll Love This Stuff! Poems from many cultures*. Cambridge University Press.

Styles, M (ed.). (1984) *I Like That Stuff – poems from many cultures*. Cambridge University Press.

AUSTRALIAN BUSH POETRY

Butterss, P & Webby, E (1993) *The Penguin Book of Australian Ballads*. Penguin Books.

Fahey, W & Seal, G (ed.) (2005) *Old Bush Songs. The Centenary Edition of Banjo Paterson's Classic Collection*. ABC Books.

Gallehawk, J. (ill.) (1991) *Australian Bush Poems*. Axiom.

Robinson, M (ed.) & Smith, C (ill.) (1999) *Waltzing Matilda meets Lazy Jack*. Silverfish.

VERSE NOVELS

Cormier, R (2000) *Frenchtown Summer*. Puffin Books.

Creech, S (2004) *Heartbeat*. Bloomsbury.

Herrick, S (2002) *Tom Jones Saves The World*. UQP.

Herrick, S (2002) *Do-Wrong Ron*. Allen & Unwin.

Herrick, S (1999) *The Spangled Drongo*. UQP.

ORAL POETRY

Agard, J, Nichols, G (eds.) & Wright, A (ill.) (2004) *From Mouth to Mouth: Oral Poems from Around the World*. Walker Books.

Cutting, L & Wilson, J (1992) *Squashed Bananas, Mouldy Sultanas – a diet of chants*. Oxford University Press.

Foster, J (ed.) & Tibbetts, T et al (ills.) (2001) *Ready, Steady, Rap*. Oxford University Press.

Harvey, A (ed.) (1995) *He Said, She Said, They Said. Poetry in Conversation*. Puffin.

Hill, S (ed.) (1993) *Jump For Joy. More Raps and Rhymes*. Eleanor Curtain.

Hill, S (ed.) (1990) *Raps & Rhymes*. Eleanor Curtain.

Hoffman, M & Cyril MC (1994) *A Rap*. Puffin.

Monkey Mark (2004) *Raps for Little Fullas*. Indij Readers.

Monkey Mark (2004) *Raps for Big Fullas*. Indij Readers.

Moses, B (ed.) (2003) *Poems Out Loud*. Hodder Children's Books.

Rosen, M & Jackson, D (eds) (1984) *Speaking to you. A collection of speaking voice poems*. Macmillan.

NURSERY RHYMES AND POEMS FOR YOUNG CHILDREN

The ABC book of nursery rhymes (2000). ABC Books.

Benjamin, F (ed.) (1995) *Skip across the Ocean: Nursery Rhymes from around the World*. Frances Lincoln.

Cross, V & Sharratt, N (2002) *Sing a Song of Sixpence – Popular Nursery Rhymes*. Oxford University Press.

Eccleshare, J (ed.) & Young, S (ill.) (1993) *First Poems*. Orchard Books.

Factor, J (ed.) & Viska, P (ill.) (1995) *Far Out, Brussel Sprout*. Hodder Children's Books.

Factor, J (ed.) & Viska, P (ill.) (1985) *All Right, Vegemite!* Oxford University Press.

Thompson, C & Viska, P (ill.) (1999) *The Dog's just been Sick in the Honda and other poems*. Hodder Children's Books.

Torres, P (1987) *Jalygurr. Aussie Animal Rhymes. Adapted from Kimberley Aboriginal Folk Stories*. Magabala Books, Broome.

Tulloch, R & Bentley, J (ill.) (1999) *Mixy's Mixed-up Rhymes*. ABC Books.

Wilcox, C (ill.) (1989) *In The Old Gum Tree. Nursery rhymes and verse for little kids*. Allen & Unwin.

Wildsmith, B (1987) *Mother Goose: A Collection of Nursery Rhymes*. Oxford University Press.

ANTHOLOGIES OF POEMS WRITTEN BY CHILDREN

Hart-Smith, W (1996) *Birds Beasts Flowers – Australian children's poetry*. Puffin Australia.

Special Forever: Uniting children across the Murray-Darling Basin. Primary English Teaching Association/ Murray-Darling Basin Commission.

The Taronga Foundation Poetry Prize (2003, 2004) *Poems by Young Australians*. Random House.

TEACHER/CHILDREN - REFERENCE AND ENJOYMENT!

Benson, G (1995) *Does W Trouble You?* Puffin Books.

Creech, S (2001) *Love That Dog*. Bloomsbury.

Crew, G & Smith, C (ill.) (1998) *Troy Thompson's Excellent Peotry Book*. Lothian.

Foster, J (ed.) (1994) *Let's Celebrate: Festival Poems*. Oxford University Press.

Janeczko, P (2002) *Seeing the Blue Between. Advice and Inspiration for Young Poets*. Candlewick Press.

Janeczko, P (ed.) & Raschka, C (ill.) (2005) *A Kick In The Head*. Candlewick Press.

Mitchell, A & Littlewood, V (ill.) (1993) *The Thirteen Secrets of Poetry*. Simon & Schuster.

Webb, K (ed.) (1979) *I Like This Poem*. Puffin Books.

AUDIO TAPES

Dahl, R (1999) *Revolting Rhymes*. Audio Puffin Books.

Fahey, W *Larrikins, Louts and Layabouts. Folk songs & Ditties from the City*. ABC Music.

Fahey, W (2004) *A Panorama of Bush Songs*. ABC Music.

Herrick, S (2003) *Tom Jones Saves the World*. Vocal Eyes.

Herrick, S (2002) *Poetry to the Rescue and more*. Vocal Eyes.

Legends of Uluru. Mastersong.

MacLeod, D read by Rubinstein, D (2002) *Sister Madge's Book of Nuns*. Louis Braille Audio.

Milligan, S (2002) *Spike's Poems*. ABC Radio Collection.

Monkey Mark (2005) *Raps for Little Fullas*. Indij Readers.

Monkey Mark (2005) *Raps for Big Fullas*. Indij Readers.

Prelutsky, J (2002) *The Frog Wore Red Suspenders*. Harper Children's Audio.

Waltzing Matilda, Songs from the Bush. ABC Audio.